"Honest, realistic! If you follow the suggestions in the fi rst part of this book, you can be on your way to financial independence".
- **Bob Bombacci**
Trust Deed Investor for over 20 years.

"Even as a seasoned investor I picked up several helpful tips from reading this book. I think every young investor should have Trust Deeds as an integral part of their portfolio and a copy of this book as well. I wish I had this book when I fi rst started to invest. I enjoyed the book very much and cannot say enough about it, except read it."
- **Rick Greenberg**
Trust Deed Investor for over 20 years.

"This book should be taught in schools."
- **John Gardner**
Trust Deed Investor for over 20 years.

"This could be the most important book you will read in your life. Amar provides a complete introduction into Deed of Trust investments that will put you on a glide path for savings and security. DOT's have proven to be better investment than the stock market with less volatility and anxious moments. A must read book to get you going in the right direction."
- **John Julian**
Trust Deed Investor for over 16 years.

"We have, over a period of more than twenty years, profited from investing in DOT's with an honest and knowledgeable broker, to enjoy a comfortable retirement in our golden years."
- **Mr. & Mrs. Leo Raiche**
Trust Deed Investors for over 20 years.

"I found the book "Make Your Money Make Money for you" very useful and informative in learning about Trust Deed Investments. I can highly recommend reading this book.
- **Michael Oliver, Esq.**

MAKE YOUR MONEY MAKE MONEY FOR YOU

A Step-by-Step Guide to Trust Deed
Investments and Financial Independence

Learn How To Get 12% Interest
On Hard Money Loans

by

Amarjit Ahluwalia

Author House books may be ordered through booksellers,
www.amazon.com, www.barnesandnoble.com or by contacting:

AuthorHouse™
1663 Liberty Drive, Suite 200
Bloomington, IN 47403
www.authorhouse.com
Phone: 1-800-839-8640

First published by AuthorHouse 9/11/2007

ISBN: 978-1-4343-1270-9 (sc)
ISBN: 978-1-4343-1272-3 (e)
ISBN: 978-1-4343-1271-6 (hc)

Library of Congress Control Number: 2007903397

Printed in the United States of America
Bloomington, Indiana

This book is printed on acid-free paper.

To my wife, Surinder Ahluwalia, who is a personification of love, giving, and acceptance, and to my children Nisha Ahluwalia, Jasjit Ahluwalia, and Amit Vyas, who bring sheer happiness in my life.

Amarjit Ahluwalia

FREE ADVICE ON YOUR
FIRST TRUST DEED INVESTMENT

Congratulations on taking a step towards financial independence! Now that you have purchased this book, forward your contact information to me and you will be entitled to free advice on your first Trust Deed Investment. You may also want to join our "TD Investment Banker" club. As a member, you will be kept posted about our seminars, investment opportunities, and also receive invitations to meet-and-greet events with other Trust Deed Investors.

Email, snail mail, or fax your Name, Address, Phone and Fax numbers and Email address to me at:

info@trustdeedinvestment.com

P.O. Box 35623
Monte Sereno, CA. 95030-0623

Fax: 408-516-8405

For more information, you may contact me at

800-935-6266 X 100

www.trustdeedinvestment.com

ACKNOWLEDGEMENT

I must thank my loving wife, Surinder Ahluwalia, for all her love and support. Thanks to my children Nisha, Jasjit and Amit for their help and support. Thanks to Attorney Javed Ellahie, for his whole hearted help on the bankruptcy chapter. I would like to thank Dan Heise of Author House for patiently explaining to me the publishing process. Special thanks to Larry Lantis and Kristi Pelzel for all their support and encouragement. Thanks to my copy editors, Nikki Royston, Deborah Riffin, and Erin Barrett. I also take this opportunity to thank Applied Business Software, for allowing me to use their forms as samples.

DISCLAIMER

The purpose of this book is to present an overview of Trust Deed Investments, and to introduce you, the reader, to a whole new way of making your money make money for you. Because theory is one thing and practice is another, this book is to be used only as a guide. Even a small, seemingly insignificant variation can make a huge difference. Consult your attorney before making any investment. All calculations, examples, scenarios, and projections are only estimates and hypothetical.

TABLE OF CONTENTS

INTRODUCTION

CLOSE YOUR EYES AND IMAGINE yourself in retirement. What does that look like for you? Are you comfortable? Traveling? Buying things for the grandkids? Whatever the picture, I'm certain the picture includes the stuff you've waited for after a lifetime of hard work.

But what is it going to cost? How much money will you be making at age sixty-five? What have you been doing — what are you doing today — to get you ready for your retirement?

If you're like most Americans, the answer to the last question is a definite, "not much." The average life of a savings account in America is less than three years and the average balance is under $4000 which doesn't allow for any medical or financial emergencies and doesn't allow for any retirement plans. Statistics show that 65% of Seniors are not financially independent and 10.2% of Seniors actually live below poverty level.[1] These people each worked very hard, all of their lives — on average 40 years — but somehow, they simply weren't able to prepare for their retirement. Stop, and think for a minute about working for 40 long years, then, barely surviving financially into retirement. Scary, isn't it?

---

[1] *65 Plus in The United States – 2005, The American Census Bureau*

Let's put it in perspective.

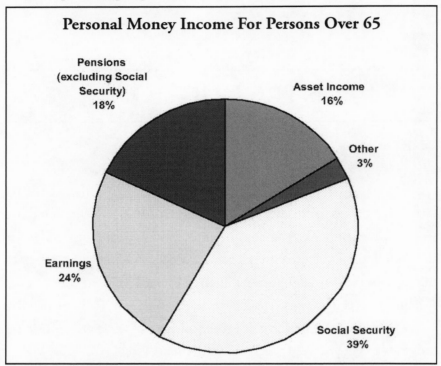

Personal Money Income For Persons Over 65

The chart above shows that on average, an American over sixty-five has a personal income heavily dependent on Social Security. Average yearly income for an American Senior is $23,787. What is the source of a Senior Citizen's income? 39% social security, 24% earnings, 18% pension, 16% asset income, 3% other. Low 16% income from assets reflects poor financial planning.

If, after all that hard work, one is still dependent on Social Security to make both ends meet, it means only one thing: working hard, 40 hours a week, even for 40 or so years, does not guarantee financial freedom.

It takes a lot more than working five days a week, for 40 years, to retire to the Bahamas, spend winters in Florida or knock the ball around at the golf club. It takes smart, careful planning.

CHAPTER 1

THREE STEPS TO

FINANCIAL FREEDOM

> NOTE: If you have zero credit card debt and have more than $25,000 in your savings account, you may want to skip to STEP THREE.

IF YOU DO NOT MAKE financial planning a serious part of your life today, then, all the hours and days you spend working will not save you from becoming a statistic; forcing you to live frugally in your old age.

Unless you start planning now, your tomorrow will not be better than today. In fact, it could be worse.

Take a good, honest look at your financial situation. If you find that, like most Americans, after working for half your life, you still won't be able to be financially independent in retirement, consider how you'd fare in the face of a financial emergency or a fiasco. It's frightening. It's truly time to wake up and realize that none of this is going to get better on its own. Wishful thinking is not going to bring a magical money fairy and you're not going to win the lottery.

With a few simple money strategies, found right here in this book, all of that is about to change. You are about to find out how to make your retirement dreams a reality. There's nothing standing between you and your dreams, except you. All you have to do is decide what you want and then, go after it - starting today.

I'm certainly not proposing a get rich quick scheme. You don't get rich quick in the real world, and you rarely get something for nothing. I'm not trying to dash every hope that you have, but, if you're waiting for the knock on your door to tell you that some rich Uncle has died, leaving you a fortune that will set you up for the rest of your life, don't hold your breath. Rarely does that ship come in real life, so, maybe you should have a solid back-up plan.

But, before we talk about how easy it really is to become rich, let's take a step back and find out why 80% of us are not rich. I figured out the answer one day, when my twenty-two year old daughter, Nisha, who was living with us at that time, came to me and asked: "Dad, I'm being offered a job transfer away from home. What do you think?"

Hm... What do I think?! It was sweet that she cared about my opinion. She had to make a decision, and she was trying to make the right one. The reality of life is that we have to make decisions almost everyday. Every decision we make, and act upon, shapes our destiny. Every decision we make, affects not only our life, but, the lives of those who are near and dear to us, and, in some cases, a lot more people than just our close circle of family and friends.

So, there I was, sitting across from my precious daughter, faced with a question, the answer to which would affect her future. Money was one factor. On her own, Nisha would have to pay for every little thing, including repairs and visits home. She was single, and would be living by herself, so, there was an issue of safety. Those were all factors I had to consider.

I knew how much it cost for me to run my household but, I wanted to crunch the numbers for her, to see if, based on her salary, the job transfer made good financial sense.

We took out a piece of paper and a pencil and started sketching it out: Rent, electricity, gas, auto insurance, food, cable, phone, laundry, entertainment, shopping, dining, etc., and the budgetary items began to pile up.

We were shocked to realize that after listing all her basic, everyday life expenses, she would have very little money left over. Keep in mind that, at the time, Nisha had no debt – no credit cards, no car loan, no student loans – and no payments, yet, after all was said and done; she would have very little money to tuck away. The reality was that whatever little she could save, would not be enough to motivate her to keep on saving. In this case, one extra purchase, a little splurging, or an emergency, would wipe out the small savings she did have, and she would be back to square one. While living with us, a major portion of her take-home salary went to savings — something that clearly, she couldn't continue doing if she moved out.

This experience was quite an eye opener. It was obvious that she would have an uphill battle, financially speaking, just like the rest of us. No wonder eighty percent of us struggle financially.

But, it got me thinking about the "why" of it. Why are things like this? Why must 80% of the people in the richest nation in the world struggle all their lives, and at the end, during what's supposed to be their relaxing, peaceful, golden retirement years, still have to live from hand to mouth? How does that happen?

I started looking into it more deeply, and here's what I discovered:

I found that just knowing the traps that led, in part, to this financial plight, was helpful in bringing me closer to understanding how to achieve financial success. It taught me, and I pass along to you, what *not* to do, as well as, what to do to become financially solvent. With any luck, once we understand that the profit-driven financial system we live in is actually working against our financial success, we can stop blaming ourselves for not being financially successful. We work hard for our money. Some of us are even working two jobs to make ends meet. Others of us own our own businesses and work all seven days of the week. But, somehow, we still find ourselves falling behind.

So, why is it like that? If we're working hard, then don't we deserve to have some financial success? Where are the rewards? What is holding us back?

STEP ONE
THE DEBT TRAP & FINDING YOUR WAY OUT

THERE ARE TWO THINGS THAT hold us back financially. One is our present salary system, which needs major reform. I am not going to talk about it in this book, as I want to stay focused on showing you how to make the best use of whatever your income is. It is not how much you make; it's what you keep that matters. And why must most us find it so difficult to keep a good portion of the money we make? That brings me to the second thing that holds us back financially: the debt trap. We fall victim to debt trap early on, and once we get caught in the debt trap, it is difficult to get out.

This is how it starts: The year you get into college, you're bombarded with credit cards. The credit card companies actually come to campuses and hand out applications to new students, who are eager for a little extra spending money. Most of us will also take out student loans to help pay for tuition, supplies, and books, and to cover a little of our cost of living. Generally, you don't have to make payments on these loans until six months after you graduate. Some folks go a step further to cover their expenses, taking out consumer loans and buying cars on credit. Needless to say, by the time you get out of college, you're already swimming in debt. Even more harmful, by the time you graduate, as a young adult, you are already programmed to borrow money and only pay the minimum monthly payments. Many of us have already completely wrecked our credit rating before we even begin our professional lives.

But wait, it doesn't stop there! After you graduate, you rush into a job – any job- so, you can keep making minimum payments on all of your debt. The cycle keeps going; you now enter the work force, where you need a new wardrobe, a new car, and your own place to live. How will you pay for these before you have even received your first paycheck? You turn to the credit card companies, again. Not surprisingly, they're more than happy to feed the need and help you incur more debt.

You have already been programmed to think about credit and debt in a certain way: If you can make the monthly payment, you can afford to buy it.

Hey, don't blame yourself too much. Do you think it's by chance that you are just out of college and already in debt? Do you think it's just by chance that you feel compelled to buy a new model car every few years? It's easy to believe that it's all benignly cultural. After all, it's the American way to keep up with the Joneses, right?

It's not by chance that the auto companies spread the financing over five years only, that they come up with new models every year, making your model look old and outdated, and the fact that the cars depreciate in value so quickly. None of this is random; it's all a well thought out marketing plan, to get you to keep buying. You are a money-making machine, not only for yourself, but for them too. The minute you get a job, you get invitations to have more credit cards. The giant credit corporations know your buying power. They know your spending habits. In fact, they know you better than you sometimes know yourself. They can predict your financial future pretty accurately, just by looking at your financial profile. They want to be a partner in your income. No wonder most all of us are always in debt.

Does it ever feel like you're working for the credit card companies or other lenders? This feeling isn't unusual, and I have news: You are. You may not be working for them directly, but indirectly there's no doubt about it. Bottom line: most of your income goes to others, in the form of interest. In addition to having to pay taxes, a big chunk of your income evaporates in interest obligations.

So, how can you save when there is nothing left over to save? The bottom line is you have to figure out how to not be a victim of the system. Instead, use it to your advantage. Credit and borrowing is not evil in and of itself. If you know how to use it to your advantage, it can be a terrific financial strategy. You can even borrow your way to riches. But here's rule number one: exceptions aside, if you are young and have no assets, then you must stop borrowing now, and start saving. When you have assets, then you can use them to borrow cheap money and invest it to make more. But the first thing you must do is get out of debt, so you can move on to Step Two: Saving.

So, is there a way for an individual born into an average family to beat the odds? The answer is a big yes, if you get on the right track and stick to it. There are many examples all around us. To go back to Nisha, her decision to stay out of debt and remain with us for a while longer, paid off. By the way, Nisha decided it would not be prudent for her to take the job transfer. That decision definitely kept her life on track. She bought her first house when she was twenty-three and her second house at twenty-six. Needless to say, A debt-free life not only has financial rewards, it also raises the quality of life for yourself and for your family.

CAN YOU DO THIS
ONE SIMPLE LITTLE THING?
GET AND STAY OUT OF DEBT

WE ALL KNOW THAT BEING in debt is detrimental to our financial freedom, yet, we keep on accumulating debt. Add up all the payments you make on your credit cards. Think about what you could do with that money, if you were not making those payments. Instead of making the credit card companies rich, you would be making yourself rich. You cannot start saving until you are out of debt.

The first goal is, don't get any deeper into debt. Do not use credit cards. If you cannot pay in cash or pay-off the bill when you receive it, don't buy it.

Second, pay-off those credit cards. List all your credit cards, with their balances and interest rates. Then, find the credit cards, with the lowest annual interest rate. Contact those companies to request an increase on your credit limit and give them the credit card numbers of all the other credit cards that you want to pay-off. Hopefully, you have now consolidated all your credit card balances into one, or maybe two, low interest credit cards.

Third, pay more than the minimum balance every month. Pay as much as you can. The goal is to have a zero balance on your credit cards. Remember, no goals, no achievements.

Fourth, make a written plan as to how you are going to systematically pay-off your credit card debt, within a specified time frame. Goals are meaningful only when you have deadlines for them.

Fifth, if you have any money in a savings account, use it to pay-off your credit card debt. It makes no sense to earn even 6% interest on your savings account, while paying 9 to 18% interest on your credit cards.

Sixth, good credit is very powerful. It amazes me when people do not take their credit seriously. I have known people who make a lot of money and yet, their credit score is very low. You owe it to yourself to spend some time paying your own bills. No one has a reason to be delinquent on a $20.00 payment and yet, this happens all the time. If your credit is not good, you are going to pay higher interest rate. That means your money is going to evaporate, in the form of higher interest. You are going to make other people rich.

STEP TWO
A SAVINGS PLAN THAT WORKS
SAVE AT LEAST 10% OF YOUR NET INCOME

ONCE YOU ELIMINATE YOUR DEBT, your focus and passion should be saving. Sound boring? Well, I'm going to make saving an easy process for you and fun too. This book will give you step-by-step instructions for a financial plan that will ensure you have a comfortable life when you retire. It will show you how to save money, and how to get past the initial pain of a limited budget, so you can start to enjoy watching your dollars grow.

Many of the calculations provided in this book are based upon an average savings of $500 a month, but, all the calculations are easily laid out, so that you can easily work out a budget for your specific situation and see your individual plan clearly. Don't assume that $500 per month is completely out of the question. It's less than $20 per day. To put it in perspective, if you pay off your car loan, just think how much money you'll have left over each month.

After I take you through the steps of understanding the importance of savings, I will show you how to take your monthly savings commitment and turn it into, not just a comfortable retirement, but, a *dream* retirement, with lots of money at your disposal.

It's human nature to ignore the simple and the obvious, thinking that the ways of the past are outdated. Remember hearing your grandparents say: "A penny saved is a penny earned?" It's a quote from Benjamin Franklin that has held a lot of truth over the generations.

You start with one penny, and coin by coin, you grow a mountain of pennies. A drop at a time fills the bucket. But, there has to be a drop, and there has to be continuity.

Saving is a slow process. To begin with, it requires a great deal of patience. Like the natural law of survival of the fittest, the toughest survive. This applies in the world of finance too. It takes discipline, perseverance, passion, motivation, fast action, and the right decisions to be financially successful. Saving is powerful enough to put you among the financially independent Americans. Ignore it, and you are like a rolling stone that gathers no mass.

So, never underestimate the power of a simple concept. The greatest individuals in history had the determination and tenacity to follow through on their ideas. Most powerful ideas are so obvious that we fail to notice them, even when they're right in front of our eyes. Until you see and understand that saving your dollars, here and there, can make you a millionaire, you won't start to move ahead.

The term "saving", is used here in the broader sense. Although using a bank savings account is in the first stages of the process, true saving is really about an entire investment plan. Learning the steps and following the plan is what will make your money grow quickly. You're going to learn how to make your savings work for you, in a low risk way. What you earn, you will keep.

First things first: As mentioned, forget about becoming rich overnight. Let's concentrate on assuring a financially secure and comfortable living, for now, and, for the future.

Let's start out slowly. No matter your age or how much money you make, begin by putting a little money in a savings account every month. Choose a reasonable amount to save, based on your income and your expenses/bills.

Take a piece of paper and write down how much monthly income you believe you'll need when you retire at, let's say, age sixty-five. Be generous with your expected monthly income. For now, don't worry about where the money will come from, just think about how much you'll need to be able to live comfortably.

Now look at the following charts. Match your present age with the amount of money you can save every month and the percent interest you can earn. From there, look how much you will have saved by the time you turn sixty-five.

Age	Savings	Interest	Total Savings at 65
30	100	7%	$181,156
35	100	7%	$122,708
40	100	7%	$81,480
45	100	7%	$52,397
50	100	7%	$31,881

Age	Savings	Interest	Total Savings at 65
30	200	8%	$461,835
35	200	8%	$300,059
40	200	8%	$191,473
45	200	8%	$118,589
50	200	8%	$69,669

Age	Savings	Interest	Total Savings at 65
30	300	9%	$889,154
35	300	9%	$368,894
40	300	9%	$338,859
45	300	9%	$201,868
50	300	9%	$114,373

Age	Savings	Interest	Total Savings at 65
30	400	10%	$1,531,310
35	400	10%	$911,730
40	400	10%	$535,156
45	400	10%	$306,278
50	400	10%	$167,169

Age	Savings	Interest	Total Savings at 65
30	500	11%	$2,486,736
35	500	11%	$1,139,663
40	500	11%	$795,290
45	500	11%	$436,786
50	500	11%	$229,428

Age	Savings	Interest	Total Savings at 65
30	1000	12%	$6,495,269
35	1000	12%	$3,529,913
40	1000	12%	$1,337,890
45	1000	12%	$999,147
50	1000	12%	$504,576

Age	Savings	Interest	Total Savings at 65
30	1000	15%	$14,860,644
35	1000	15%	$7,009,820
40	1000	15%	$3,284,073
45	1000	15%	$1,515,954
50	1000	15%	$676,863

All the above calculations are simplistic. The whole purpose is to show you the power of savings. Of course, you are not going to get

10% interest on your $1000 deposit, but, let it grow to $20,000 and you will; once you invest that in Trust Deeds. You can also calculate the accumulation of a savings plan that's personalized for your specific situation, by using a financial tool, like the HP12C calculator, for example.

$100 A MONTH SAVINGS FOR 35 YEARS		
		DISPLAY ON SCREEN
To Clear Calculator		
Enter: f CLX		0
Number of Years		
Enter: 35 g n		420
Interest Rate		
Enter: 7 g i		0.58
Monthly Contribution		
Enter: 100 PMT g Beg		100.00
Future Value after 35 Years		
Enter: FV		**$181,156.08**

In our world, we're geared to think in terms of a lump sum, and our ability to spend it all at one time — to live "high on the hog," as it were. It's far more beneficial to think in terms of your desired monthly income, after retirement.

If you're thirty years old and you can save $500 a month at 10% interest, by the time you're sixty-five, you will have approximately $1,914,138. Now, think in terms of what the interest income on $1,914,138 would be at 10%. That comes to $191,413 annually, which translates into $15,951 a month in interest income. At age 65, you can live off this interest, without ever touching the principal balance of $1,914,138. If you are able to get a 12% interest rate on the same money, your monthly income would be even higher, to the tune of $19,141.

If you're thirty-five now, and can save $500 a month at 10% interest, then you will have accumulated $1,139,663 by age sixty-five. At 12% interest, your monthly income will be $11,396. How does that compare to your current monthly income from your job? No matter what your present financial situation, initiating a simple investment strategy, that yields at least 10% interest, will make you a winner in the end.

The chart below shows the calculations in black and white. For example, if you want to save $500,000 by the time you're sixty-five, and you are receiving 12% return on your investment, you'll need to put away $143.06, as shown below:

	DISPLAY ON SCREEN
To Clear Calculator	
Enter: **f** **CLX**	**0**
Number of Years	
Enter: 30 **g** **n**	**360**
Interest Rate	
Enter: 12 **g** **i**	**1.00**
Future Value of $500,000	
Enter: 500,000 **FV** **g** **end**	**$500,000.00**
Your Monthly Contribution	
Enter: **PMT**	**$143.06**

Again, 12% interest income on your savings of $500,000 will give you a $60,000 annual income or, $5000 a month; without doing anything! These are the financial rewards of prudent planning.

If you already know a little about bank savings, you may be wondering how you'll get a 10% interest rate (much less 12 %!) on your savings account. Most savings accounts don't give a return nearly that large. Most of them only offer a 2-6% interest rate.

This book will show you how to take your savings out of the bank, away from their low, low, interest rates, and transfer it into an investment vehicle that safely provides a return of 10%, or more. Instead of making $800 a year in interest income (based on $20,000 in savings), you can now make a minimum of $2000 a year in interest income. Over the course of twenty or thirty years, this translates to a huge difference in earnings from the typical bank account.

As discussed, your savings may start slowly, but, it will multiply exponentially, in due time. The trick is to actually initiate a savings plan, no matter how small, and then, stick to it. You must save at least 10% of your family's monthly net income. The best way to save is to take 10% of your salary right off the top, with an automatic payroll deposit into your savings account from each paycheck. Most financial institutions offer this service, free of charge. If, for some reason, this is not available, you can easily do a manual transfer of 10% or more, from your checking account to your savings account. Do it faithfully, do it regularly, and do it *right now*. This will set you on the right path. If you get paid weekly, then deposit weekly. It's always easier to deposit in small amounts. But, whatever your pay schedule, get in the habit of making your savings deposit part of the routine. The trick is to not lose the continuity.

If you break the mold of the average American; if you're smarter than your neighbor; you will initiate and execute a savings plan and you will persevere. If you do this, you will be rewarded with a lifetime of luxury and financial freedom, to do whatever you wish. You've got to be smart. You've got to be persistent and you've got to be good. Throw yourself into this challenge. Head down to the bank and open your "Golden Years" account.

Is $500 a month too much to save right now? Not a problem. Put aside whatever you comfortably can, but, just save. Your first priority, if you owe money to credit card companies and have a car payment, is to pay them off. Once that's done, and you no longer owe, you will free up a lot more money for savings each month. Soon, you will be able to come up with a savings amount you can live with.

But, here's the catch: if you overestimate how much to put into savings, you may be cutting yourself off at the knees. On paper, it may look like you can afford to put aside $400 per month, but, if in order to do that, you would have to cut out the things you have gotten used to, and enjoy, that will soon leave you pretty discouraged. A small example would be going to your favorite coffee place in the morning for cappuccino. You do not want to give that up for anything. Giving up small things in life that you enjoy, is not going to make you rich. If anything, that is going to de-motivate you. Human nature being what it is, if you have to give up your morning cappuccino to save a few bucks, you might do it for a few days, but, eventually, you will go back to your cappuccino; and when you do that, you will give up on the whole savings plan too. The trick is to have a realistic plan. The amount you choose to save each month has to be easily doable. The very first time you have difficulty depositing the selected amount, you will be tempted to give up on the whole plan. Start low. Nothing is more defeating than making goals you can't stick to.

So, if you think you can save $400 a month, start with $300 instead. After a few months, if you still feel strongly that depositing

$400 a month will work, increase it. Remember, also, that nothing is stopping you from putting more into the pot some months than you have allotted. However, if you have a little extra once in a while, also consider spending it on yourself. Take a break. Go to a nice restaurant. Take a mini vacation. Splurge a little; spoil yourself. Just as tomorrow is important, today is important, as well. Spend that little bit of extra money on whatever makes you feel good about yourself. Having a balanced life is always an imperative. A savings plan is just like a diet: if it's too painful, then you will quit.

Remember, this account is set up for one thing only: to provide you with monthly income when you retire. You never, ever, dip into the account. A good way to remember is the catchy phrase, *the golden rule for the "Golden Years Fund" is money goes in and doesn't come out."*

The game has begun. Make no mistake; it will be a test of your discipline and willpower, especially at first. When you know you can win, you have already assured yourself a place among the fortunate few who are financially independent at retirement. You have guaranteed yourself, and your family, the sweet taste of financial freedom. You, in fact, are a very successful and smart individual. Keep your eyes open; stay alert; watch for the tricks your mind is going to play on you and never, ever, dip into the "Golden Years Fund".

Now stop. Put this book aside. Figure out how much you can comfortably save each pay period, and then knock it down by another 20%, just to assure your success.

Now that you've done that, it's time to open the account. Not next week or next month, but today. Even if you have to knock off work a little early — do it! It is a *must* that you give yourself this deadline. This is your first test.

By doing the above, you have already taken the first step toward achieving financial independence. Congratulations! This is what's called mature financial planning. Looking at money dispassionately and in a grown-up way is not as easy as it seems. So, give yourself a pat on the back for having taken these first few steps. At the end of this book, you will see a new you — a confident, financially stable person, who others look to for money advice.

Now, we're going to follow up with the third step to financial freedom: Acting on, and sticking to, your financial plan, which translates into making your money make money for you.

> ## *Time + Savings + High Rate of Return = Financial Success.*

STEP THREE
MAKE YOUR MONEY MAKE MONEY FOR YOU

NOW IS THE TIME TO learn what others already know, but haven't told you. It's safe, secure, and you'll watch your money grow at a controlled pace.

What I am going to show you is a simple and straight-forward method to accelerate the growth of your money, yet, very few people ever think of it. The reason for this is because people, who use this method of doubling their money, don't often talk about it. The fact is, a very small, exclusive community of investors is raking in huge profits, and the bottom line is: they don't want any competition.

Who are some of the biggest revenue generators in the world? The banks. How do banks, credit unions, and insurance and finance companies make their money? By loaning money and charging interest. Financial institutions have been generating riches in interest income since the beginning of time. So, why can't you? What do they know that you don't?

Amazingly, the business of money lending has gone beyond just the banks. Casinos, home improvement stores, airlines, internet companies, and virtually every large retail outlet in America, are issuing their own credit cards. Try to pay cash at a furniture store, and they'll do anything they can to talk you out of it. They want you to put it on account, and they're even willing to give you a year to pay it off, interest free, to get you to do it. Of course, when the interest does kick in, it will be at 23%. You could end up paying three times the cost of your purchases by the time you pay it all off. Obviously, they don't want your cash today, because, if they wait a while, they'll be able to get much, much, more from you; by charging you high interest on your purchase.

These companies are making money by making their money do the work. They've discovered the power of doubling.

There is an old story about a King, who loved to play the game of chess with his favorite Minister. One day, the Minister played an excellent game and the King was thrilled. The King was so impressed and pleased with the Minister's game, that he told the Minister he could have anything he wanted.

"Ask for anything," the King said to the Minister.

"I am a poor man," said the Minister, "All I want is to make sure that my family and I have enough food to eat. So, if Your Honor is really so pleased, how about giving me some grain?"

"How much grain do you wish to have?" the King asked.

The Minister looked at the chess board and said, "Only a little. Just put a grain in square one, two grains in square two, four grains in square three, and so on, until the last square, number sixty-four. "

The King was shocked. "That's all?" he asked. "Well, consider it done."

And, the King called his Food Minister and told him to fulfill the Minister's wish.

Does the Minister's request sound simple or too low? Initially, yes, but, if you stop and think about doubling the amount of grain in each square, the total grows exponentially; very quickly!

CHAPTER 2
THE DOUBLING GAME

THE INCREDIBLE POWER OF DOUBLING

1	2	4	8	16	32	64	128
256	512	1,024	2,048	4,096	8,192	16,384	32,768
65,536	131,072	262,144	524,288	1 mil	2 mil	4 mil	8 mil
16 mil	32 mil	67 mil	134 mil	268 mil	536 mil	1 bil	2 bil
4 bil	8 bil	17 bil	34 bil	68 bil	137 bil	274 bil	549 bil
1 tri	2 tri	4 tri	8 tri	17 tri	35 tri	70 tri	140 tri
281 tri	562 tri	1 quad	2 quad	4 quad	9 quad	18 quad	36 quad
72 quad	144 quad	288 quad	576 quad	1 zil	2 zil	4 zil	9 zil

OBVIOUSLY, THE KING COULDN'T FULFILL his Minister's wish without bankrupting the kingdom's food supply. But, this example shows the incredible power of doubling. If you get the best rate of return, the rest is just a time game. And, that's how financially successful people grow their assets.

Simply put, here's what the banks do. They borrow money from consumers, people just like you, in the form of deposits. Then, they lend that same money out as mortgages, lines of credit, credit cards, auto loans, personal loans, and commercial and business loans. The banks take your deposits, give you a low interest rate, and then, turn around and loan the deposits to someone else, at a higher rate of return. The difference between what they pay out to you in interest on your savings account, and what they charge a borrower, is the profit they make.

Literally, you deposit your money and get anywhere from 2% to 6% on your savings account. The bank then turns around and loans your money to people like yourself, and businesses, at interest rates varying from 8% to 18%, and puts the difference in its pocket, to cover the operating costs of doing business and to make some profit. The good news is that if the banks can do it, you can, too.

Let's assume that you've been on your savings plan and you've saved $20,000 but, have been getting only about 4% interest. Wouldn't you like to start getting 10% interest — more than double what you have been getting so far?

So, how do you invest the same $20,000 safely, and earn $2000 in interest income per year, rather than just $800?

You get into Trust Deed Investments. When I talk about Trust Deed Investments, I am also talking about Hard Money and Private Money Loans. Trust Deed Investments are made mostly in Hard Money loans. Private Money is used to fund Hard Money

Loans, which are also known as Trust Deed Investments. So, if you understand Trust Deed Investments, you also understand Hard Money Loans.

What exactly is a Trust Deed? A Trust Deed is a written instrument, legally conveying property to a trustee, often used to secure an obligation, such as a mortgage or a Promissory Note.

The Deed of Trust, which is recorded with the County Recorder's office, involves three parties:

1. A lender or the beneficiary
2. A borrower or trustor
3. A trustee, which is a third, neutral party (generally, a Title Company).

In a Deed of Trust, the borrower transfers the property, in *trust*, to an independent third party (trustee), who holds conditional title, on behalf of the lender or investor (beneficiary). The Trustee can then:

1. Re-convey the deed once the loan is paid off; and or
2. Sell the property should there be default (foreclosure).

A Trust Deed can be a First, Second, or a Third mortgage, depending on when it was recorded in the chain of recorded deeds on a particular piece of property. When buying a home, a buyer typically puts down 0 to 20% of the purchase price, and the bank finances the balance. The borrower (buyer) signs a Promissory Note to repay the loan at a certain time, in a specific number of installments, and at a certain rate. The Promissory Note contains other conditions like late charges, prepayment penalty, acceleration clause, etc. This Promissory Note is secured by a lien on the borrower's house. This voluntary lien is called a Trust Deed, or a mortgage, and is recorded with the County Recorders office, in the county where the property is located. In this case, the bank is the first one to record its Trust

Deed with the county recorder's office, so, it's dubbed "first Trust Deed."

Let's say that the owner then takes out a $50,000 home equity loan. This will be considered a second mortgage, "junior lien" or "second Trust Deed."

If, after a while, the owner decides to pay off both the first and second mortgages to get a new loan, this loan will now be a first Trust Deed again.

But, back to you: You'd definitely like to invest $20,000 in a Trust Deed Note for five years at 12%. Twelve percent is reasonable in Hard Money loans, and it's not a difficult market to break into. This book will walk you through the process of getting into Hard Money loans, step by step, but first, let's take a look at the numbers and start getting excited about the financial possibilities that lie ahead.

Assuming you earn 4% interest from the Bank. Your investment of $20,000 will grow into only $64,867 in 30 years. At 12% annual interest, your investment of $20,000 can grow into almost $600,000, within thirty years. At 15% your investment of $20,000 can grow into $1,325,000, in the same period of time. Just 3% extra makes such a huge difference. You can actually double your money every five years with a 15% return! Remember, all these figures and calculations are estimates. The idea is to bring to your attention the huge amount of money you lose when your money is earning only 6% or so in interest.

You can calculate exactly how long it will take to reach a certain dollar amount. Let's say that you want to invest $100,000 and can get an 18% return. To find out how long it will take you to double your money to $200,000, use the following formula on your HP12C calculator. You will find that it takes only 5 years to double your $100,000.

DISPLAY ON SCREEN

Clear Calculator

Enter: f $\boxed{\text{CLX}}$

Present Value of Savings

Enter: 100,000 $\boxed{\text{PV}}$

Interest Rate

Enter: 18 $\boxed{i}$

Future Value of Savings

Enter: 200,000 $\boxed{\text{CHS}}$ $\boxed{\text{FV}}$

How Many Years To Double Savings

Enter: $\boxed{n}$ **5 years**

This same $100,000, invested in a simple CD account with your bank, would probably earn at a 4% interest rate. It would only grow into a meager $121,665 in five years. You would actually lose $78,335 by investing your money in a CD account. When you add an average inflation rate of 5%, plus Uncle Sam's share, you may barely have made any headway at all.

It's not the bank's fault. They can't afford to pay you more than 6%, or the given market rate, at any given time, because the bank has to make its own profit to stay in business. They have to invest at a higher rate to cover overhead and show profit to their shareholders.

It's easy to forget, before you've taken the path of doubling your money, that the money in your savings account is *already* invested in all sorts of loans, including billions in credit cards. The banks do this with your money, everyday. By playing the Trust Deed game yourself, and investing directly, you eliminate the middleman (the bank), and reap *much* bigger rewards (your profits).

The Doubling Game

So, HOW DOES ALL OF this play out? Well, let's see. Using your financial calculator, take $20,000, invested over twenty years, at 15% interest, and compute:

$20,000 INVESTED FOR 20 YEARS AT 15% INTEREST	DISPLAY ON SCREEN
Clear Calculator	
Enter: f CLX	0
Number of Years	
Enter: 20 n	20
Interest Rate	
Enter: 15 i	15
Present Value of Investment	
Enter: 20,000 PV	20,000
Future Value in 20 Years	
Enter: FV	**$327,330**

Your answer is a future value of $327,330! This is after 20 years and only starting with a mere $20,000.

Now, let's plug in some different numbers.

$20,000 INVESTED FOR 30 YEARS AT 15% INTEREST		
		DISPLAY ON SCREEN
Clear Calculator		
Enter:	f	CLX
Number of Years		
Enter:	30	n
Interest Rate		
Enter:	15	i
Present Value of Investment		
Enter:	20,000	PV
Future Value in 30 Years		
Enter:	FV	**$1,324,235**

Now, let's take this even one step further. What if your Note has a prepayment penalty clause for the first year? A prepayment penalty clause means that if the borrower pays off the loan during the first year of its term, the borrower will pay a prepayment penalty of six months interest, on the remaining 80% of the loan balance. The prepayment penalty is always based on 80% of the balance. Since this is a simple interest-only loan, 80% of $20,000 is $16,000. You would take fifteen percent of $16,000, which is $2400. Divide that by 2 to arrive at six months interest. That gives you $1200 in pre-payment penalty, paid to you. Let's say the borrower pays off the loan in six months. In this case, you collect $1200 in interest, plus $1200 in a prepayment penalty, for a grand total of $2400.00. The final return on your money: A sweet 18%.

Go ahead, and get excited! Before, it was going to take you thirty years to reach your goal; now, it will take you only twenty. You just jumped ahead by ten years!

That's the power of doubling. Get the best rate of return, and the rest is just a matter of time.

Now that you know it's possible to double your money faster, set some specific and realistic goals to do so. Later, you can expand on them, but first, you need to understand the principles and rules of this new game that you're about to play. For starters, let me assure you that returns in the range of 10% to 15% or more, are easily possible with Trust Deed investing, and with minimal risk.

But, where can you find these rates? Here's a brief overview of the process. Later, I will walk you through many of the steps in greater detail.

CHAPTER 3

GET A MORTGAGE BROKER

THE FIRST STEP IS TO find a good mortgage company that deals in Hard Money Loans on daily basis or, a Trust Deed Investment company you can trust. There are plenty of them out there.

Another option is to invest through mortgage pools and REITs (Real Estate Investment Trusts). In REITs you can buy units to suit your financial situation, instead of waiting for a Note to come available. Each unit is generally $5000. REIT's mostly invest their money in big construction project developments. They also invest in commercial buildings like shopping centers, malls, office complexes, and rehabs. With a Mortgage or a Trust Deed Investment company, you can fund a loan all by yourself or join others. When you join others, these are called fractionalized loans. The minimum investment is determined by the size of the loan, and by how many investors the Mortgage Broker wants to put in that particular loan. In cases like this, where you are a part investor, the mortgage company holds on to the original Note and

Trust Deed and you get a copy. The Mortgage company collects the monthly payments, and then, disburses them.

If you are the hands-on type, and would like to get more involved in each of your investments, then funding a loan by yourself is ideal for you. In this case, you have all the control and you make all the decisions. You will find out what you prefer, depending on your individual personality, as you begin to fund a few Trust Deeds. You can find Trust Deed Investment and Mortgage companies specializing in Trust Deed Investments and Hard Money loans by going to the almighty Internet or your local newspaper. Go to an online search engine like Google or Yahoo. Plug in "Trust Deed Investments" and take a look at web sites like www.trustdeedinvestment.com. Also, try your local newspaper, under the Money Wanted, Trust Deeds, or Mortgages for Sale section.

Find a good, Hard Money Mortgage Broker, and take his opinion seriously, as he has first hand information about the borrower. Hopefully, he knows the business. A Mortgage Broker — especially a responsible and prudent Mortgage Broker — will give as much weight to willingness and the ability of the borrower to pay, as he will to the equity in the property. A responsible Mortgage Broker will turn down a 40% LTV loan if making that loan could cause the borrower, the broker, or the investor a heap of trouble. Maybe the borrowers are an elderly couple, with not enough income to make the mortgage payment, let alone other expenses. A responsible broker would never jeopardize his clients, the lender, or himself. A broker has many options and will have the house professionally appraised, the borrower's credit checked, income verified, and all the ratios worked out. A good Mortgage Broker knows as much about the borrower, as he knows about the property. A good Mortgage Broker knows that dealing with a good and responsible borrower, will save a lot of headache later on. He does this for your protection, as well as, his. Should anything go wrong, it's the Mortgage

Broker's license on the line. It's important to work with an ex Hard Money Mortgage Broker who has been closing and se Hard Money Loans for private investors by himself, and not throu using other Hard Money lenders. A good Mortgage Broker can save you a lot of hassle and can help you make a lot of money.

Always check the company's resume. Here are some good qualifying attributes: You're looking for a local mortgage company, with at least ten years of experience funding Hard Money loans. You'll want at least three solid references, also. Check with the investors who have invested money in Trust Deeds with that company for at least ten years, not with the competition. You may also want to talk to the Title Company they deal with. However, nothing compares with your personal experience. Even the very first deal you get from a Mortgage Broker, will give you a great insight into him. You can tell if a Mortgage Broker is focused only on making his commission, or, if he is passionate about this business. Just what he gives you, and how he presents the investment to you, will give you great insight. If, upon review, you find out that all the comparables (comps) in the appraisal he gave you are ridiculous, then you know he is not the guy you want to deal with. Or, if the property is in really bad shape and the appraisal does not reflect that, and the loan to value ratio is at 70%? Then, you know he is not for you. What if you end up owning a property that is too far away or too far in disrepair? If, after reviewing the package, you see that funding this loan will put the borrower in a worse situation and there is no way the borrower can make the payments, it does not make sense to do the loan. What would make this loan even worse is if the borrower is a senior citizen. The Mortgage Broker should be looking out for you, and for himself, and should not even submit a loan like one of the above examples, to you. There will be many other indicators, as well. You find out all of this by your own personal dealings with the broker, and by talking to other

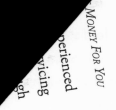

dealt with over the years. Bottom line: there is
~~personal~~ ersonal experience with the broker. Start with
hance to show you his work, his expertise, and
it from there. Remember, you are not making
~~oaning~~ to a third party. You, your Mortgage
Broker, Appraiser, Escrow Officer and the Title Company, are a team.
It is a fun business and a great way to make your money make money
for you, if you have the personality for it.

Next, the mortgage company will ask you about your criteria for
investing in Hard Money loans. Here are some sample questions you
should be prepared to answer:

- Do you only want to invest in first mortgages or will you
  take either first or second mortgages?
- Do you want to invest only in properties located within
  50 miles of your residence, or, will you invest statewide or
  even nationwide?
- How much money do you want to invest at this time, and
  what type of properties do you want to loan money on?
  What is the maximum Loan to Value (LTV) ratio you will
  go to?
- Are you willing to join others, or, do you want to be the
  only lender on a loan?
- Do you want the mortgage company to service the loan, or,
  do you want to service it yourself?
- *Most Mortgage companies charge between half to one percent
  fee for servicing the loan. So, if the borrower is paying 11%
  interest, your net could be 10.50% or 10%.*

You can also invest by buying an existing Trust Deed, through a
Mortgage Broker or a private party. All the requirements are the same,
except, in this case, everything is already done. You get the original

Note, original Deed of Trust, assignment of Deed of Trust, appraisal, copy of senior Note, 104.1 endorsement of the title insurance policy, copy of recorded request for notice of default, fire insurance loss payee and Lender/Purchaser Disclosure Statement of existing Note.

In a case like this, the transaction itself is very simple. All the escrow company has to do is issue an endorsement and record assignment of the Deed of Trust, and you become the proud owner of the Trust Deed Note. Once that's done, then congratulations are in order. You're now making double the money you were making before, when your money was kept in bank.

CHAPTER 4

Evaluating A Note

So, you have found a mortgage company you like and they have sent you an investment sheet on all the Hard Money Loans they have available for you to consider investing money in. The investment sheet has the following information:

- Property Address
- Property Profile
- Market Value
- Mortgages/ Liens on Property
- Monthly Payments
- Loan amount the borrower is requesting
- Whether the new loan will be a first or second mortgage
- New loan term
- Loan to value ratio
- Protective Equity
- Rate of Return

So, what do you do with all this information? You answer these questions:

- Do you like the location?
- Do you like the type of property?
- Is the dollar amount in your range?
- If not, do you want to join other investors?
- Is the loan-to-value ratio good with you?
- Is the protective equity good with you?
- Is the position of Deed (First or Second) good with you?
- If it is Second Deed, can you handle the payments on the First, in case of default?

Remember, these are just some of the questions. Let's say that everything seems good. In that case, you will call the mortgage company and let them know that you're interested, and you would like to review the complete package on the investment. While the complete package is being delivered, you may want to drive by the property, if it's within driving distance. This way, you know exactly what the property and neighborhood are like. Its fun to see the property for yourself, plus, it gives you more confidence going into the deal. Occasionally, there have been situations where a potential investor, doing research on a property, discovered items the appraiser wasn't even aware of.

Once you decide to fund the loan, the mortgage company will provide you with the Lender/Purchaser Disclosure Statement, which will give you all of the information on the borrower, the Trust Deed, and the property. In addition, you can also request copies of the following items, so, you can know more about the borrower and the property:

1. Loan Application
2. Credit Report
3. Appraisal
4. Preliminary title report

5. Lender/Purchaser Disclosure Statement
6. Fire insurance information

If you are making a second mortgage, you will also need the following: a copy of the First Mortgage Statement and the Note. If the borrowers cannot locate the First Mortgage Note, which is not unusual, the mortgage statement, combined with the credit report, may be enough, provided that the mortgage statement gives you plenty of information about the loan, like its interest rate, term, balance, etc. Most importantly, you want to make sure that the first mortgage loan is a 30 year loan and does not have a balloon payment that comes due before your Note. If it is an adjustable rate mortgage, you want to know when and how much the rate and payments will go up. These loans may have substantial rate increases when the fixed rate term on these loans has expired. The typical fixed rate time frame on these 30 year loans is anywhere, from 2, 3, or 5 years. Most Mortgage Brokers and Investors do not go behind another private investor loan. If the first mortgage information is not available at all, the Mortgage Broker or Title Company can get a beneficiary statement from the senior lender. The beneficiary statement will reflect when the loan was originated, who the borrower was at the time of origination, the interest rate, term of the loan, next payment due date, late charges incurred, any prepayment penalty, balloon payment, and additional advances, as well as, if the loan has any negative amortization added to the present balance.

One thing you always have to take into consideration when making a Trust Deed Investment, is whether or not you would like to own the property, should it happen to fall into your lap. You can answer this question by deciding if the property is easily marketable, or how much rent you might get for it? If you're funding a second mortgage, you must also consider if you would be able to bring the first mortgage current, if the borrower falls behind. Everything about the first mortgage is important and applicable, if you're investing in a second mortgage.

LOAN-TO-VALUE RATIO (LTV)

THE LOAN TO VALUE RATIO is calculated by taking the total of all the loans owed on the property, and dividing it by the property value. If there is only one loan on the property, the ratio is called Loan To Value (LTV). If there is more than one loan on the property, then you take the total of all the loans, including your own, and divide it with the property value, to arrive at combined Loan-To-Value Ratio (CLTV).

For example, let's say the market value of the property is $100,000. The first mortgage balance is $50,000. You are making a second loan (your Trust Deed) of $20,000. That means the total combined loans against the property are in the amount of $70,000. Now, divide $70,000 by the total market value of $100,000 to get your CLTV ratio of 70%.

Example: 70,000 / 100,000 = 70% CLTV

Or, let's say the market value is $100,000. The first mortgage is $25,000. The second mortgage is $15,000. You are making or buying a third Trust Deed, in the amount of $25,000. The total of all three loans combined is $65,000. You divide $65,000 by the total market value of $100,000, which gives you a loan-to-value ratio of 65%.

Example: 65,000 / 100,000 = 65% CLTV

The equity of a property is the difference between the market value and what is owed against it. If the market value is $300,000, and the first Trust Deed or initial mortgage is $150,000, then the homeowner's equity is $150,000. However, for Trust Deed Investment, an investor looks for lendable equity — a percent of the total — rather than full equity. A private investor never wants to finance an entire home 100%. There's simply no protection. Banks make loans up

> **Combined Loan-To-Value Ratio: The total loans against the property, including your loan, divided by the market value and expressed as a percentage.**

to 100% of the market value only because these loans are insured, and banks, frankly, have broader shoulders. They can risk taking a loss, and do take losses, but, those losses are absorbed. Banks depend on the overall return on their billion-dollar portfolio, not just the return on one investment.

So, how do you calculate lendable equity? Let's take this example; the market value of a property is $300,000 and the borrower's already have a first mortgage loan of $150,000. Previously, you have already decided to only make loans with a maximum lendable equity of 70%. The total equity in the borrower's home may be $150,000, but, the lendable equity is only $60,000. Here's how we calculated it.

Example calculations	
Market value (MV):	$300,000
70% of Market value:	210,000
Minus first trust deed:	(150,000)
Lendable equity:	60,000
Equity:	150,000

If you want to loan only up to 65%, then you can loan $45,000.

As a rule, stay with 65% or less LTV. The lower the LTV ratio, the more protection you have. More equity in the property gives the borrower more incentive not to lose his home. Also, it gives him room to borrow more, in case he falls behind in his payments. You never want to be the last lender on a property, unless you want to

> **RULE!**
> **STAY WITH 65%**
> **OR LESS LTV**

own the property. You always want to have an exit strategy, well laid out, before you even make the loan. Always leave room for someone else to pay you off.

LTV RISK FACTORS	
0-65%	None
65-70%	Low Risk
70-75%	Fair Risk
75-80%	Very Risky

Bottom line: the lower the LTV or CLTV, the less the risk. The accuracy of your LTV or CLTV ratio depends on the accuracy of the appraised value of the property. Therefore, it's very important to determine the market value of the property accurately: not high, not low, and just accurate.

DETERMINING THE MARKET VALUE

THE SINGLE MOST IMPORTANT ASPECT of smart Trust Deed investing is accurately determining the market value of a property.

There are Three rules to remember:

Rule One
Just because a property is listed or being sold at a certain price, does not mean that it is really worth that much.

Rule Two
Just because a property is appraised at a certain value, does not mean it can be sold at that price.

Rule Three
An appraisal is an opinion of an appraiser based on market comparables and adjustments, and it can sometimes be off.

Most people skip down to the bottom of an appraisal to find out what a property is worth. To be an informed, savvy investor, you'll need to review the entire appraisal. Read the appraiser's comments and look closely at the comparables provided. Here are a few items you should take into consideration:

1. Make sure the subject property is compared with similar or like properties. A 2000 square foot home with three bedrooms and two bathrooms should always be compared to another 2000 square foot home with three bedrooms and two bathrooms. At the very least, the square footage should be

very close. You cannot compare single family homes to cluster or duet homes. You can, however, compare a three bedroom, two bath home, to a three bedroom, one bath home, but, only if an adjustment is made for the one bath, and, it is risky. This is where you have to consider the marketability of the property. If, or when, the market is slow, it will not only be hard to sell a three bedroom, one bath home, but, it could also drop in value, more than the appraiser's adjustment. Take a look at all of the adjustments to ensure they make sense.

2. Make sure all of the comparable properties in the appraisal are in the subject property's market area, and that all of the comparables are on closed sales, within a maximum of six months.

3. Do your own research. You will be surprised how much you can find out now-a-days on sites like zillow.com. Of course, there is nothing like actually driving by the property, and contacting some real estate agents who have listings in that neighborhood. Sometimes, a dividing freeway or, even a street, can make a huge difference in the selling price. In a slow market, the house that backs up, or fronts to a busy street, may sell for a lot less than the appraised value. In another case, it may be the school district that increases or decreases the value of a home.

4. Make sure the street address of the subject property on the appraisal report is correct, and matches the address on the Preliminary Title Report. Also, that the APN number on the appraisal matches the APN number on the Preliminary Title Report.

There are several different kinds of appraisal forms. Some Mortgage Brokers use short forms, some use Fannie Mae Forms, and some can provide you with comparable sales from a Title Company or from a multiple listing service. As long as the information provided is accurate and makes sense, you will be fine.

Debt Ratios: Does the Borrower Have the Ability to Make the Payments?

Even though a lower LTV or CLTV gives you more protection, it's not the only consideration. You have to think about the borrower's ability and willingness to pay on your loan.

If late payments and filing foreclosures do not bother you, you will make a lot of money in Trust Deeds. But, if you want your payments to be on time, and have no hassles with chasing delinquent borrowers, then, you may also want to look closely at the quality of the borrower, instead of relying solely on the equity in the property. You may, or may not, get the top return. That is, if the going rate is 12%, you may get loans at 10%, but, you may end up with fewer headaches in the long run. Nobody can predict the future, but, if you play it a little safer by choosing dependable borrowers, you will have a better chance at the loan being a good one, even if the interest on it isn't as high. Having said that, the fact of the matter is the rate of return in Trust Deed Investments seldom has anything to do with the risk. Consider this: You fund a $100,000 loan at 9% interest at 65% Loan To Value ratio, and there is an equity protection of, let's say, $200,000. If the exact same loan was written at 12%, would that make it riskier? Most people pay higher interest rates for the speed, and convenience, and for the fact that it is just a short term or band-aid loan.

So, the loan may be written at 12% and yet, be a perfect loan, and the borrower may never miss a payment. The higher return, as explained before, has nothing to do with the quality of the loan, as long as the loan is made properly and meets all the underwriting guidelines. The reason a borrower sometimes pays a higher return is not because he has bad credit, but, because he needs the money fast and without too many hassles.

A perfect example is a young businessman, one who's been in business for, let's say, only a year and a half. He doesn't have a proven track record to show to the bank. He's going to have to pay a little bit more in interest for his first loan.

Most people who invest money in Trust Deeds, to fund hard money loans, are either middle aged or retired. Typically, these people have had some financial success and are now ready to take it easy. They have no desire to own more real estate and deal with management hassles. They invest their money in Trust Deeds, with the idea to get the best possible return, safely, and without market fluctuation. They want a smooth process, which will enable them to receive their payments on time. The last thing they want to do is to foreclose and repossess a property. So, the big question in their minds is: Will the borrower make the payments and make them on time?

The answer to this question is found in the borrower's credit report and debt ratio.

In hard money lending, the debt ratios, if any, are pretty liberal. Generally speaking, if the borrower had the debt ratios required by the bank, he wouldn't be going for a hard money loan in the first place. On the other hand, he could have excellent debt ratios, but, bad credit.

Most investors don't even ask what kind of work the borrower does, let alone the borrower's income. Nonetheless, it still pays to know how to calculate the debt ratios and understand why the banking industry debt ratios are so stringent; making many perfectly responsible borrowers unable to qualify for a loan. In defense of lending institutions, they have to be stringent, due to regulations they are required to follow, and because they are making loans at higher loan-to-value ratios, upwards of 80 to 100%. You'll be able to see the bank's loss as your gain, as you begin to gain confidence in Trust Deed Investments.

The underwriting criteria, whether it is you or the bank that is making the loan, is the same: borrower's ability and willingness to pay-back the loan. The borrower must have the ability to make the payments.

Banks and other conventional financial institutions all have their own formulas to determine the borrower's ability to make loan payments, using either debt ratios or discretionary income.

> **Discretionary Income:**
> The money left over after all bills have been paid.

For first mortgage loans, most lenders accept debt ratios of 33 %(front) and 38 %(back). That means that a borrower's total housing expenses including principal, interest, taxes, and insurance, should not be more than 33% of the borrower's gross monthly income. The back end ratio, which includes not only the house payment, property taxes, and insurance, but, also includes installment payments like personal loans, auto loans, and credit card payments, should be no more than 38% of the gross monthly income.

Think about it for a second and you'll realize how strict these ratios are. With today's high real estate prices, very few people can really qualify with those ratios. As a result, many lenders are becoming more creative and liberal with their underwriting guidelines. I've seen conventional lenders make loans with backend debt ratios as high as 60%. With the bank's more creative and liberal guidelines, if a borrower puts down 20% or more as down payment, he can get a "no income check" loan from a bank. If a person has decent credit, he can get a "no income verification" refinance loan to 80% loan to value ratio.

As a new investor, your concern will most likely be whether or not the borrower has enough resources to make the payments. As you become experienced, however, you will find that Trust Deed investors don't even look into debt ratios. They're strictly going on the basis of equity in the property. Their logic is that if the borrowers had qualifying debt ratios, they would not be going for private money loans. This may make sense for their particular goals and with their years of experience and instinct, but, you may want to ask yourself: why make a loan to someone you know can't pay you back? There is a very thin line here, and this is where the experience comes in.

People who invest money in Trust Deeds or fund hard money loans, just want their monthly interest checks paid on time. If they wanted to buy real estate at bargain prices, they would just do that by going to auctions. So, it's been very critical, at least in my experience, that unless the borrower is selling the property or has some money coming from somewhere, he or she must have the income to make the payments.

You'll need to decide what criteria will have to be met before you lend your money. As long as you stay informed and open to possibilities, you'll be fine.

CREDIT

DEBT RATIO SHOWS A PERSON's ability to pay, but, as an investor, you should also take a look at their willingness. What do I mean? From the look of some people's credit, they just don't seem to want to pay their bills. Whether or not a person has the willingness and ability to meet their financial obligations, is indicated by the kind of credit they have. Never underestimate the importance of a borrower's willingness to pay. Some people may not understand how the credit system works, and end up having bad credit. But, there are lots of people out there who do have an understanding of the system and have an excellent credit score, despite unbelievably high debt ratios. This is due to a high motivation and willingness to pay their bills, even in difficult financial times. Because of this fact, Fannie Mae started buying no income verification loans, based on a borrower's excellent credit score.

Making proper use of a credit report comes with experience. It is like reading into a person. It's like knowing a person well enough that you can almost predict his paying habits. If the credit report shows chronic slow pays, then, of course, he's a slow payer. With a borrower like this, you will always have to expect his payments late, but realize that, he does still pay.

There are some people who will never pay unless you call

> **Charge Off:**
> The lender wrote the debt off and took a loss

them. If you see recent charge-offs on the credit report, that's indicative of a person having major financial problems. Always take the time to find out how the borrower pays on his home mortgage, regardless of how he pays (or doesn't pay) his other accounts. You may have a borrower that always pays his mortgage payments, and, even if they're late, they're made.

Look for this important insight in your borrower's credit history. The mortgage payment should always come first, followed by car payment, and then, the credit card payments. Some borrowers will never be late on their mortgage payment, whereas, they may be late with all the rest of their bills.

While looking at their credit and financial situation, you are also calculating their potential for bankruptcy. If the credit is not good, you might prefer to loan them 65% instead of 70%. Maybe, you want to cut the loan down to 50% LTV. There are many ways to take a potentially weak loan, and turn it into a doable loan. Always look for a way to make the loan.

Regardless of how much importance you or the mortgage broker give to the credit and debt ratios in any given hard money loan scenario, it is always better to go into something knowing everything, no matter how bad, than to go into something knowing nothing at all.

CHAPTER 5

PUT UP THE MONEY

ONCE YOU HAVE REVIEWED ALL the facts about a particular property, and have decided to make the loan, the broker will do the rest. He serves as your representative, from here on, out. All you have to do is to wait until the Title Company calls you for the funds.

When it's time to pay, you'll need a cashier's check, made payable to the Title or the mortgage company. When you go to the Title or the mortgage company with your cashier check, they will show you the entire loan package. Review it to make sure that everything is accurate. Your Mortgage Broker and the Title Company are responsible for every little detail, as they are licensed people, getting paid to make sure that every "I" is dotted and every "T" is crossed. These professionals are there to protect your investment. Make sure everything in the papers is to your liking.

As a lender, you can communicate directly to the Title Company, or your broker can do it, on your behalf. Either way, make sure that all of your requests and instructions are followed. If you are funding the package, you get the original Note, plus copies of the Deed of Trust and evidence of fire insurance, etc. The Title Company does not disburse the loan proceeds until the Deed of Trust is recorded at the county recorders office. It usually takes about thirty to forty-five days to receive the original recorded Deed of Trust back from the County Recorder's office. In the meantime, however, the Title Company can provide you with a copy of the Recorded Deed of Trust, until the original arrives. This also applies to requests for a copy of Notice of Default, and a request for Notice of Delinquency, or any other document that needs to be recorded.

THE FUNDING PACKAGE

THE FUNDING PACKAGE CONSISTS OF the following:

1. A Copy of the instructions to the Escrow Company. This tells you exactly what position your loan is in, and what items on the Preliminary Title Report are being paid off, deleted, or staying.
2. Estimated HUD 1 / Settlement Statement. This shows you how the loan proceeds were distributed.
3. The Original signed Note
4. A Certified Copy of the Deed of Trust
5. A Certified Copy of Request for Copy of Notice of Default and Request for Notice of Delinquency
6. The Preliminary Title Report
7. Fire Insurance loss payee with your name as Beneficiary or lender. Make sure the policy offers replacement cost, or, is enough to cover all loans on the property.
8. A Copy of the Loan Application
9. A Copy of the Rental Agreement, if it is a rental property
10. The Homeowner Association address and phone number, if it is a condo or townhouse
11. The Lender/Purchaser Disclosure Agreement
12. Servicing Agreement

You may already have some of these documents, prior to funding the loan.

CHAPTER 6

PUMP UP THE PROFITS!

Now THAT YOU HAVE A basic understanding of the Trust Deed Investments, let's focus on several ways to maximize your profits.

MAKING MONEY ON MONEY
YOU DON'T EVEN HAVE!

LIKE MANY AMERICANS, YOU'RE PROBABLY real estate rich, and cash poor. Let's assume that you own real estate that's currently worth more than what you owe against it, meaning you have lendable equity. Provided your credit's good, you can borrow against this equity in your home. That's good, because right now your equity is like cash lying in the basement of your home, just collecting dust.

You can borrow at a good rate of interest for 15 years or even for thirty years. Then, you can turn around and invest that money in Trust Deeds at a higher interest rate. The difference is your profit. You're doing exactly what the banks do.

Let's say that you can borrow $50,000, at 7% fixed interest rate for fifteen years, at a monthly payment of $450.00 (the numbers are rounded for simplicity). You turn around and invest the same amount at 12% interest, for five years, at interest only payments of $500. You can make your monthly payment of $450 and keep the balance of $50 in your pocket, or reinvest it.

Most of these short term, Trust Deeds have prepayment penalties. So, if your Trust Deed Investment gets paid off early, your return can jump higher than 12%. Even without the benefit of a prepayment penalty, and assuming that you keep your money invested at 12%, you will make a profit of $59,000 in fifteen years — almost $4000 a year in income.

Work the numbers yourself: In fifteen years, your $50,000 mortgage will be paid off, with someone else doing the paying. It is the same as with your rental property, where your tenant is paying your mortgage payment. So, now, you not only have the $50,000 you originally borrowed from the bank and invested in Trust Deeds, but you also have $9000 you collected in extra interest.

Do this right, and you'll build a fortune using the equity in your home. I know some investors who have been doing this for years.

BUYING DISCOUNTED NOTES

DISCOUNTED NOTES DON'T COME AROUND everyday, but, when they do; the returns they provide are phenomenal.

> **Carry back loan:**
> A loan in which a seller agrees to finance a buyer in order to complete a property sale.

So, what are we talking about? You can buy Trust Deeds at a discount. You're looking for a seller with a "carry back" Trust Deed Note. Most sellers who carry back a Trust Deed on the sale of their properties, do so reluctantly, and really have no idea what to do with these Notes. The small monthly payment does not excite them and, more often than not, they spend all the cash proceeds from the sale of their house. They remain cash poor, looking around for more money.

To clarify, let's create a hypothetical scenario. Mr. and Mrs. Sellers is an elderly couple. They want to sell their home. When they list their home, they're told that it would sell within ninety days or less. Ninety days go by and they don't even get a nibble.

They lower the asking price and finally receive an offer. The only problem, it's not an all cash offer. The real estate agent convinces them that since they're going to put most of their proceeds into a savings account anyway, they might as well help the buyer by carrying back a Note, which is called a "seller carry back" (or "seller carry back paper"). Reluctantly, they agree. This is what the transaction looks like:

Purchase price:	**$200,000**
Cash down payment:	**56,000**
Buyer to assume 1st Trust Deed:	**124,000**
Seller to carry back 2nd Trust Deed:	**20,000**

Mr. and Mrs. Sellers agree to carry back the $20,000 Note for five years, at 10% interest. The monthly payment is interest only at $166.67, with a balloon payment of $20,166.67, at the end of five years.

The retired couple moves out of town, but, a few months later, Mr. and Mrs. Sellers need about $15,000 to pay off a hospital bill Mr. Sellers accrued last month. They go to their neighborhood bank, but, unfortunately, because they no longer own a home, the bank turns them down for a loan.

In the meantime, Investor Mike, who deals in buying discounted Trust Deeds, comes across information about this $20,000 Trust Deed from the County Recorder's office. Knowing, from his experience, that five years is long enough to motivate any Note holder to sell at a discount, he mails them a letter, stating who he is and that he can help them cash in their Note. Because the Sellers really need the money, and by this time, are very frustrated, they jump at Investor Mike's offer.

Mike gets all the information over the phone.

"Five years, that is like waiting forever. How did you accept such a term?" he asks.

The Sellers tell him that they didn't know any better. Investor Mike says he will look over the figures and see if there's a way to make it work out.

He gets off the phone and takes out his calculator. He's looking to make at least a 20% return. Mike jots down the following information on a worksheet:

•	**Interest rate:**	**10%**
•	**Original balance:**	**$20,000**
•	**Current balance:**	**$20,000**
•	**Payment Structure:**	**Interest only**
•	**Current payment:**	**$2,000 annually**
•	**Time remaining on loan:**	**4 years**

Mike gets his financial calculator out and punches in the following information:

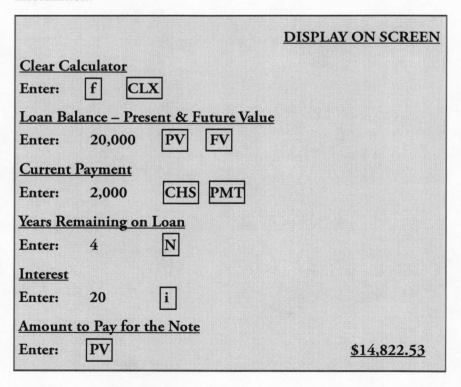

DISPLAY ON SCREEN

Clear Calculator
Enter: f CLX

Loan Balance – Present & Future Value
Enter: 20,000 PV FV

Current Payment
Enter: 2,000 CHS PMT

Years Remaining on Loan
Enter: 4 N

Interest
Enter: 20 i

Amount to Pay for the Note
Enter: PV   **$14,822.53**

The price to pay for the $20,000 Note is $14,822.53. Investor Mike calls them back the next day and offers them only $14,000. Mr.

and Mrs. Sellers are, of course, taken aback, but Mike lets them know that he has to borrow the money from the bank at a high interest rate, and the only way to justify the cost and make the whole deal work is to buy the Note at that price. The Sellers tell him that they need $15,000, minimum, and Investor Mike says that he has only $14,800, cash. If they can take the original Note and the Deed to the Title Company first thing in the morning, they have a deal. The Sellers agree.

Nothing is, of course, in writing yet, and Mike can take a little more time to look at the Note and the other relevant papers. If he's satisfied, he will go ahead with the transaction of buying the Note, and end up with a 20% or more return on his investment. In the end, the Sellers have won by being able to pay off their bill. Mike has won too, with a profit.

CREATING AN INCOME STREAM

INVESTOR MIKE NOW HAS THE option of either keeping the Note or, turning around and selling it. Let's assume that Mike knows an investor who loves to buy good Notes and is happy with a 14% yield. Mike calls him, gives him all the information, and the investor is willing to buy. Let's figure out the purchase price at 14% yield:

	DISPLAY ON SCREEN
Loan Balance – Present & Future Value	
Enter: 20,000 PV FV	
Current Payment	
Enter: 2,000 CHS PMT	
Years Remaining on Loan	
Enter: 4 N	
Interest	
Enter: 14 i	
Amount to Sell Note for	
Enter: PV	**$17,669.03**

Mike sells the Note to this investor for $17,669.03. How much did Investor Mike make for writing a letter and making a few phone calls? A cool $2,869.

Now, let's be even more creative. Mike could have bought this Note with absolutely nothing from his pocket. After making the deal with the original Note holder, Mike could have opened escrow and instructed the escrow to assign the Note to his investor friend, who will bring in the cashier's check for $17,669. The Title Company cuts the check to the note holder for $14,800 and cuts you a check for the difference of $2,869. Not bad for a few hours of work.

How about still another example of creativity. Let's say that Mike has no investor readily available to buy the Note from him, and somehow, Mike has no money to purchase the Note himself. Mike, being a seasoned Note buyer, goes to his friendly thrift institution and gives them photocopies of all the documents. The thrift institution agrees to lend Mike $14,800, with the Note as security. Mike instructs the Title Company that he is receiving the loan and gives them the appropriate instructions. Mike just bought the Note by taking a loan against the Note itself, or hypothecation.

Guess what happens in six months? The Note gets paid off. After paying off the thrift institution, Mike walks away with $4200.

When you are buying a Trust Deed Note from a mortgage company, you know the rate of return because it's spelled out in black and white on the Note itself. But, what if you're buying an existing Trust Deed, at 10% interest, and you want a 15% return? How do you figure out what price to pay for the Note? In order to do that, you'll need your financial calculator again.

The first thing is to know what yield or return you want on your investment. We'll work with a 15% return. The Note you are considering buying has the following information:

•	**Interest rate:**	10%
•	**Original balance:**	$20,000
•	**Current balance:**	$20,000
•	**Payment:**	$166.67 per mth interest only
•	**Months remaining:**	24

To calculate how much to pay for this Note, so your yield is 15%, use the following procedure:

				DISPLAY ON SCREEN
Loan Balance – Present & Future Value				
Enter:	20,000	PV	FV	
Current Payment				
Enter:	2,000	CHS	PMT	
Years Remaining on Loan				
Enter:	2	N		
Interest				
Enter:	15	i		
Amount to Sell Note for				
Enter:	PV			**$18,374.29**

The purchase price for this Note should not be more than $18,374.29 to yield you 15% interest.

Familiarize yourself with this calculation, because it will come in handy.

Now, let's look at another example, where the current balance is not the same as the original balance.

The Note you're considering buying has the following data available:

•	**Interest rate:**	12%
•	**Original balance:**	$20,000
•	**Current balance:**	$14,056.12
•	**Payment:**	$420.36 per month
•	**Amortization:**	5 year fully amortized
•	**Months remaining:**	36

How much will you pay for this Note in order to net a yield of 16%? Use the following simple functions on HP-12C:

	DISPLAY ON SCREEN
Current Payment	
Enter: 420.36 [CHS] [PMT]	
Current Balance – Present Value	
Enter: 14,056.12 [PV]	
Years Remaining at 12% Interest	
Enter: 3 [G] 12 [X]	
Yield of 16% over the Current 12% Interest	
Enter: 16 [G] 12	
Amount to Pay	
Enter: [PV]	**$11,956.64**

The price to pay for this Note is $11,956.64, which will get you approximately a 16% yield.

Most of the time, you will be dealing with interest only short-term loans, but, with the above example, you now know how to figure out the desired yield in a fully amortized Note.

When you find a deal like this, jump on it! Even if you don't have the cash yourself, find the cash – the rates of return are just too good to pass by.

How Fast You Want Your Money to Grow

Once you have done the groundwork, and know the kind of Trust Deeds to buy and which broker to go through, the big question is: At what rate and how fast do you want your money to grow? Even though the money market conditions and the supply and demand control how much return you can get on your investment, you do have some control over it.

Never let a high rate of return scare you into thinking that it may be a high-risk Note. The return is high mainly because of the easy money and the speed with which a Mortgage Broker can fund a home equity loan.

Bottom line: it's the equity in the house that you are banking on. Would you be willing to loan me $100,000 if I give you my $125,000 to hold on. You bet! If I don't pay you $100,000 back you can keep my $125,000. That's exactly what you are doing when you loan someone a mortgage on their house where the protective equity is mostly equal to or more than the money you are loaning them. Take for example:

Value of the Subject property:	**$1,000,000**
First Mortgage balance:	**$400,000**
Your New Second Mortgage:	**$200,000**
Total owed on the property:	**$600,000**
Protective Equity:	**$400,000**
LTV:	**60%**

In this case, your $200,000 is secured and backed by $400,000 equity in the subject property. If your loan was for $250,000 the protective equity would have been $350,000 and LTV would be 65%.

If a borrower doesn't pay, he has equity to lose. The smart investor knows how to see the whole picture and can move the fastest, to make the most money.

The following chart will show you the growth of your money, at different rates of return:

$50,000 invested in Trust Deeds at 10% rate of return	
5 Years	$80,525
10 Years	$129,687
20 Years	$336,374
30 Years	$872,470
$50,000 invested in Trust Deeds at 12% rate of return	
5 Years	$88,117
10 Years	$155,292
20 Years	$482,314
30 Years	$1,497,996
$50,000 invested in Trust Deeds at 15% rate of return	
5 Years	$100,567
10 Years	$202,277
20 Years	$818,326
30 Years	$3,310,588

It is clear that if you are under 35 you have time on your side. Start saving and winning is just a matter of time.

Let's see how fast $100,000 will grow if invested in Trust Deeds:

$100,000 invested in Trust Deeds at 10% rate of return

5 Years	$161,051
10 Years	$259,374
20 Years	$672,749
30 Years	$1,744,940

$100,000 invested in Trust Deeds at 12% rate of return

5 Years	$176,234
10 Years	$310,584
20 Years	$964,629
30 Years	$2,995,992

$100,000 invested in Trust Deeds at 15% rate of return

5 Years	$201,135
10 Years	$404,555
20 Years	$1,636,653
30 Years	$6,621,177

CREATE TAX FREE INCOME AND PAY-OFF A 30 YEAR MORTGAGE IN 15 YEARS BY USING YOUR HOME EQUITY

You've borrowed $100,000 against the equity in your home, at a 7% fixed rate, for thirty years. You turn around and invest that $100,000 in Trust Deeds, at 11.00% interest. Your monthly payment on the $100,000 loan is $665.30 but - this is the amazing part - interest income on your $100,000 Trust Deeds Investment is $916.66. You make a profit of $251.36.

Now, imagine this: instead of pocketing the profit from your investment, you apply the $251.36 toward the payment on the borrowed $100,000. Instead of paying $665.30 you pay $916.66. You'll pay off the $100,000 loan in just fourteen and a half years. In the meantime, your borrowed $100,000 is still sitting intact. At 12% return, you will pay-off the $100,000 loan in less than thirteen years. At a 15% return, it will take you only nine years to repay the $100,000 you took out.

In any case, by using the equity in your home, you will have earned a tax free income of $100,000 in a maximum of fourteen and a half years. That's $6,896 tax free annual income for doing absolutely nothing. Remember there is no tax on a loan. You've scored!

Pay-Off a 30-Year Loan in
Just 15 Years or Less!

Continuing with the example from the previous chapter, let's assume that in fourteen and a half years you actually paid off the $100,000 loan. The $100,000 you invested in Trust Deeds remains free and clear, providing you with an additional income of $1000 a month. What a fabulous way to create extra income for yourself! Let's take that a step further. The same $100,000, if invested for another twenty-one years, at 12% interest, will grow into a whopping $1,000,000!

Let's look at yet another scenario. Here's what could happen in thirty years if you make the $665.30 payment from your personal income and use your borrowed $100,000 to invest in Trust Deeds at 11% interest, re-investing the interest income.

1. Your $100,000 loan will be paid off in 30 years, and
2. The $100,000 loan proceeds will grow into a staggering $2,289,229.65

Your total pay off on the borrowed $100,000 (with interest over thirty years), would be only $239,508. Subtract $239,508 from $2,289,229 and you have a net profit of $2,049,721. That comes to $68,324 annually - a creative chunk of annual income.

One more item to consider: when you retire on this plan, your annual income, even at 11% interest on $2,289,229 will be $251,815.

That's $20,984 a month, without touching your principal. That will help make retirement easy, won't it?

Mind boggling, but true! And totally possible.

Time + Investment + High Rate of Return = Financial Success.

Learn How to Create $16,000 a Month Retirement Income By Saving $500 a Month

Let's assume that you are 30 years of age, and can save $500 a month. By the time you are 35, you will have a little more than $30,000 in the bank, including interest. For our purpose, and to keep things simple, we will use $30,000.

It is now time to invest that $30,000 in Trust Deeds, making 12% interest, while you keep on-track with your savings plan of $500 a month. Now, you have $3600 additional income a year, from the $30,000 invested at 12% interest. In addition, you are also adding $6000 a year to the pot. By the time you are 40, you will have $18,000 in interest income, another $30,000 from your monthly savings plan, and your original $30,000 investment in Trust Deeds, totaling $78,000! Leave that invested in Trust Deeds until you are age 65 at 12% interest, and you will have accumulated $1,326,000.

Adding $500 a month, from your own income, to your savings, for the next 25 years, even at a modest interest rate of 5%, will give you an additional $298,995. Add this to your $1,326,000 in a Trust Deed, and you will have $1,624,995 for retirement. At 12% interest, that will give you $194,999 in annual interest income or, a monthly income of $16,249. Of course, in real life, this number could be a little more or a little less.

If you want to save, let's say, $500,000 in the next 30 years, and you know you can get 12% return on your savings, the chart below tells you how much to put into your "Golden Years Fund" each month.

	DISPLAY ON SCREEN
Number of Years	
Enter: 30 g n	360
Interest	
Enter: 12 g i	1.00
Future Value of Investment	
Enter: 500,000 FV	500,000.00
Enter: g end 8	500,000.00
Monthly Contribution	
Enter: PMT	**$143.06**

Again, 12% interest income on your savings of $500,000 will give you an annual income of $60,000. This means you will have $5000 a month of additional income, just in interest alone, without lifting a finger. These are the financial rewards of prudent planning!

CHAPTER 7

UNDERSTANDING YOUR
TRUST DEED INVESTMENT

WHY WOULD ANYONE PAY 12% INTEREST?

So, WHY WOULD ANYONE PAY 12% interest if they're a good credit risk? Although we've been talking about higher debt ratios and less then perfect credit, there are people who are a good risk on paper, but, who end up taking a Hard Money Loan for one reason or another. The major reason is the strict lending policies of the Federal National Mortgage Association (FNMA) and the banks. For example, let's say that Buyer Bob buys a property for $125,000. He puts down $45,000 and the bank gives him a thirty year loan of $80,000, secured by a first mortgage on his property. The loan is made at 9.75% per annum at $687.32 per month, including principal and interest.

Nine months have gone by, and Bob's home has appreciated 10% and is now worth $137,500. Using a financial calculator, we find out that Bob's loan balance is now $79,531.58.

Bob wants to improve his home, so, he decides to take out a home equity loan to build a new pool for his family. He goes to his neighborhood bank and fills out a lengthy loan application, along with dozens of other papers. The loan officer gives Bob a long list of items the bank needs to process his loan application. The list consists of Bob's last two year's tax returns; his last month's pay-check stubs; proof of the source of money he used for his down payment; etc.

The loan officer informs Buyer Bob that the bank will order an appraisal, open an escrow, and get his loan application processed, in the next thirty days. A few days later, Bob mails out his whole life history to the bank. While Bob waits, he begins to wonder why the same bank that loaned him $80,000 less than a year ago is having such a problem giving him a small, $20,000 loan, especially when he has plenty of equity left in the property.

A week later, the appraisal is finally done, and Buyer Bob has finally checked off everything on the bank's long list. But, guess what? The new loan processor at the bank submits the whole loan package to the underwriter, who takes one look, and turns it down flat. Why? The loan officer and the loan processor had overlooked one simple bank policy that could have saved poor Bob a lot of time and effort. If a borrower owns the property for less than twelve months, then the bank will loan up to 75% of the purchase price, not the appraised value. The rookie loan processor had figured it like this:

Appraised value:	**$137,500**
75% of appraised value:	**$ 103,125**
Minus first mortgage Balance:	**(79,532)**
Loan amount available:	**23,593**

But the underwriter calculated it this way:

Purchase price:	**$125,000**
75% of purchase price:	**93,750**
Minus first mortgage:	**(79,532)**
Loan amount available:	**14,280**

The bank, then, had to turn down Bob's loan request.

Bob has already made all the plans for the swimming pool, though. His family is excited, and he's not about to let the bank throw cold water on all of his plans. He gets on the phone and calls a Mortgage Broker. In less than ten days, Bob has a second mortgage loan of $20,000.

Buyer Bob called ABC Mortgage Company, knowing that they also deal in Hard Money Loans. ABC Mortgage took all the relevant information over the phone and passed it on to one of its investors. This is how ABC Mortgage presented the loan to its investor:

Appraised value:	**$137,500**
1st mortgage balance:	**$79,532**
New 2nd Trust Deed:	**20,000**
Total encumbrance:	**99,532**
Loan to Value:	**72%**
(99532 - 137500 = 72%)	

The LTV ratio is a little high, but, the borrower's excellent credit, verified income, and the purpose of the loan, offsets the high LTV ratio. The swimming pool will also add value to the property.

The loan terms are 12% interest, for a term of five years, interest-only payments, with a balloon payment at the end of the five years.

Now, meet a new player in this tale. Investor Mike, who is familiar with the area, likes the investment and gives his O.K to the mortgage company to buy the Note. The Mortgage Broker draws up all the papers, meeting all legal requirements, and sends the documents to the escrow company. The escrow company draws up their papers and has the borrower come in and sign the loan documents. The escrow officer also explains the terms of the loan to the borrower. After the borrower has signed, investor Mike goes to the Title Company looks over all the documents and, if everything is as he was told, hands over a cashier's check to the Title Company. After the three-day rescission period is over, the Title Company records the deed; distributes the loan proceeds; and the loan is closed.

The escrow is closed and Investor Mike just became a lender. Because the bank is such a big entity, and is bogged down with so many federal, state, and internal policies, it was unable to make a relatively sound loan. It allowed Investor Mike a window of opportunity. He beat the bank, and came out ahead.

If Borrower Bob, however, doesn't make payment on his loan, Mike can foreclose and repossess Bob's new home. If that happens within two years, Investor Mike can make a $37,968 profit in equity, which comes out to a near 190% return on his investment of $20,000. Chances are, though, Buyer Bob's not going to let that happen. He values his home and is taking out the loan for improvements. He'll do all he can to make sure he continues to protect his investment.

There are other reasons borrowers are willing to pay higher interest. Some people, even though their credit is not that bad, do not even try to go to a bank. It is less intimidating for the borrower to go through a Mortgage Broker as the Mortgage Broker makes the process lot easier and convenient. It is, however, incumbent upon the Mortgage Broker, to get the lowest possible rate and fees, at the best possible term, for his borrower. So, a broker should always try to get any borrower a conventional loan, first.

Still, another reason is that a borrower is self-employed and it's hard for self-employed people to provide accurate income verification. Some self-employed people also skip getting a business license, which is a *must* if one is to get a traditional bank loan. As such, they may not qualify for a bank home equity loan.

Sometimes, a borrower needs money very fast and has no time to go through the lengthy bank process, or, the borrower needs money just for a year or two, or, even less — a bridge loan — and figures it's worthwhile to pay a little higher rate of interest, than go through the aggravation with a bank.

Yet, another category is a person who has perfect credit, but, also has a new business. Let's say Buyer Bob is an engineer, but, didn't know it would be better to get the loan before quitting his job and starting his own business. Most banks won't give you a loan if you've just quit your job and have a new business. In this case, you'd have no choice but, to pay a little more in interest. Does the fact that the borrower is paying 12% make it a bad loan? Absolutely not.

Hard money loans are also used for construction projects, land loans, mixed use properties, commercial properties and cross-collateralized properties that do not meet bank guidelines.

Most often, a person needs a Hard Money Loan because of a credit or income problem, such as being behind in mortgage payments; foreclosure; bankruptcy; tax liens; judgments etc. A lack of mortgage history can also be a reason. On occasion, an individual inherits a property and has no track record of making mortgage payments. Sometimes, the property does not qualify, is in the middle of construction or remodeling, or, is on the market for sale. Or perhaps, the borrower is between jobs. Possibly, the property is owned by a corporation or by a non-profit organization. The borrower is buying a commercial property and even though he is putting 40% down he cannot get the bank loan because the property is only half occupied or because his credit is not that great. It always amazes me. Forty percent is a lot of down payment. Well, the good thing is that Hard Money Loans are available, based on common sense underwriting.

Simply because a loan is written at 12% interest, does not mean it's a riskier loan. Don't waste too much time trying to figure out why people do what they do. If somebody's willing to pay 12% interest, then take it.

Trust Deed Investment is the same thing as investing in real estate. The bank has confidence in real estate, in fact, the savings and loans, banks, and the FNMA have so much confidence in Trust Deed Investment that they take their customers' money - customers just like you - and invest it in Trust Deeds.

As we discussed earlier, when you deposit your money in a CD account, using your favorite bank, at 3% interest over five years, you're actually loaning your money to the bank. The bank turns around and loans your money to someone else, at a much higher interest rate. The margin is their profit. When you consider the billions of dollars invested in Trust Deeds each year, you can imagine what that margin of profit might look like. Most lending institutions, fund in the billions.

Bottom line: The banks invest in Trust Deeds – you should invest in Trust Deeds. A properly originated Trust Deed, secured by a desirable piece of real estate at 65% loan to value or less, is probably one of the safest and most stable investments one can make, to make their money make money for them.

How Secure is My Investment?

When you invest in Trust Deeds, you never, ever, have to go to your computer first thing in the morning to find out how your investment is doing like you do for your stocks. Is it up, or is it down? Never! Your investment is stable; securitized and immovable. It is not going down. It only goes up, giving you interest income, all or part of which, can be put back into your investment to make it grow further.

Accidents happen on the road, in the water, and in the air, everyday, and they can happen to you. Whether you're the driver or a passenger; whether it's your fault or not, accidents do happen. Does this mean we should stop driving, flying, or even leaving our homes?

Similarly, if you invest money there's always an element of risk involved. With Trust Deed Investments, while the reward is high and consistent, there is still an element of risk — but, it's risk that you control. The best part about Trust Deed Investments is that unlike stocks and mutual funds, the risk factor does not depend on market conditions or market fluctuations. It depends on you and the Mortgage Broker. It depends on how proper; how thorough and how good a job is done on evaluating and doing a Note. You, or, the mortgage company doing the Note, controls the risk.

Questions To Ask:
- Is there an appraisal;
- Does the borrower have the ability to make payments;

- Are the loan disclosures and loan documents accurate, timely, and in total compliance;
- If you are doing a second mortgage, is the first mortgage current or being brought current in the escrow? Have you, or the mortgage company, verified in writing, the balance, monthly payment, terms and status of the loan;
- If you are involved, have you read the escrow instructions and agree with them;
- Is the Title Insurance Policy good and comprehensive;
- Are you the loss payee on the Fire Insurance Policy;

Once these questions are answered and analyzed correctly, your risk factor is miniscule. The worst that can happen is the property can go to foreclosure, but, even that is a rare occurrence. If that should happen, most likely someone will buy the property at a trustee's sale and you'll get paid off — every penny, including the late charges, the foreclosure costs, etc.

If no one buys the property at auction, then you'll end up owning a property, at probably at least twenty-five percent below market value. Instead of a 12% interest return, your return could jump to 200%!

The catch, of course, is that the Trust Deed was created correctly, which means that the Mortgage Broker, or whoever was responsible for originating the Note, did their job right.

How Liquid is My Investment?

Your Trust Deed Investment is not considered a liquid investment, but most get paid off before five years. Who wants to pay 12% interest one day longer than they have to? If you're just starting out in Trust Deed Investments and think you may need money before the due date of the Note, then you had better invest in short term Notes, that usually span only one or two years. You can also talk to the Mortgage Broker before you buy a five-year Note, and ask him if he would be able to assign the Note to another investor if you needed your cash. You'll have to pay for assignment and recording fees, but, this will be your best bet if you need to sell the Note fast at no discount.

The broker, himself, may just buy the Note from you and keep it for himself, or assign it to another investor. Other resources that you can always contact are other Mortgage Brokers that do private money loans, other investors, or friends and family members who would like to make 12% interest. Another option would be to talk to your local bank to see if they would loan you money against the Note. It is called Note hypothecation.

If it's a good Note, and the borrower is paying on time, you should be able to sell it. Don't call traditional Note buyers, who buy discounted Notes to make money. They operate by picking up deals from desperate sellers at deep discounts.

Once you find someone who's willing to buy the Note from you, everything else can be handled quickly by the Title Company, which will act as the neutral party and as trustee.

CHAPTER 8

TROUBLESHOOTING

DELINQUENCY

YOU HAVE NOW BOUGHT A Note. If the mortgage company is servicing the loan on your behalf, then that's one less thing for you to have to take care of. The only concern you have is to take the check to the bank, unless you have automatic deposit set up for the payments. Even if the Mortgage Broker is servicing your Note, you will keep the original Note, the Recorded Deed of Trust, and any assignments, unless the Note is fractionalized.

If you're servicing the Note, you may also want to inquire with your bank to see if they could collect the payments for you. Many banks collect payments for their clients either free of charge, or, for a nominal fee.

If you are servicing the loan yourself, and the borrower does not pay the late charge, don't fret. You can always collect these fees at a later date, when the borrower decides to pay-off the Note, and you get a demand from the Title Company. It is important for you to keep thorough records of payments and delinquencies, and keep the borrower informed.

Also, if you are servicing the loan, you will have to fill out mortgage rating requests and issue pay-off demands. Most of your pay-off demands will come from title companies. With your demand, the Title Company will also ask you to include the original Note and Deed of Trust, duly signed by you, to be mailed to them. You may, however, want to consider not mailing the original documents. It may be okay with the Title Company if you just mail them your pay-off demand, along with an attached letter, stating that you will deliver all original documents once the Title Company has your check ready.

When you are servicing your own Note, you must comply with all the laws. California law provides that on all balloon payment loans, the lender must give between 90 to 150 days advance notice of a balloon payment due date. If you do not give the advance notice, and the borrower does not pay off the loan when it is due, you will need to give him notice and wait out the period, before you can foreclose. The notice simply states the date that the loan balance is due, including the principal, the interest, and where the pay-off should be mailed.

At times, you will come across borrowers who pay late almost every month, but, they also pay the late charge every month. Instead of getting upset, be happy for the extra money. However, the first time a borrower is late more than ten days, call the borrower, or, send a letter stating that late payments will affect his credit and cost him more. Also, advise the borrower that if they are going to be late again, that they will need to notify you right away.

If the borrower is more than thirty days late, then send them a letter clearly stating that you need payment immediately, and, if you do not receive payment within ten days, a foreclosure will be filed. If no payment is received within the ten day deadline, and you have not heard from the borrower, do not attempt to call or send written notice again. It is time to file foreclosure.

Your own personality plays a big role in handling a customer who chronically makes late payments. The important thing is to not let yourself get stressed out over it. Your investment should be a pleasant experience for you and not a stressful one. For that reason alone, it is worth it to let the professionals service your Note.

Foreclosure

When to File and How it Works

We all know that accidents do happen and yet, no one ever stops commuting or traveling. If you invest money in Trust Deeds, sooner or later you'll be faced with a situation where you'll have to foreclose. It's really nothing to be worried about. The only person who should be worried is the borrower. The only thing you, as an investor, have to be concerned about is filing the foreclosure. Not so much the process, but, when to file it. Timing is very important.

Technically, you can file foreclosure after the payment has been delinquent for more than thirty days, but, most lenders will wait until the borrower is two payments behind. Before beginning the foreclosure process, talk to the borrower first, and make sure you've exhausted every other option. Look at the whole picture. Is there enough equity in the property to allow the borrower to refinance? Consider giving the borrower extra time to refinance. You could even recommend him to another, more aggressive lender, or, have a lender call him to discuss refinancing as an option. Once you have chosen to file foreclosure, the borrower's chances of refinancing become slim.

On the other hand, if there's not enough equity in the property, then time is of the essence, and you need to move fast. If you are interested in the property and don't mind owning it — either to sell it or to rent it out — and, if the borrower's willing to sell it to you, take the property by *deed in lieu of foreclosure*. If you do end up taking the property by *deed in lieu of foreclosure,* make sure that you go through the Title Company. It is a good idea that the borrower is represented by an attorney and everything is documented. This way you are completely protected if the borrower is hit with remorse, changes his mind, and tries to go back on the deal, or, comes back to you later, accusing you of taking undue advantage of his situation, and pleading total ignorance.

When you take a property "in lieu of", you may have the right to assume any and all senior liens. You can review the senior lien Note yourself, or, have your attorney do it. This should be done sooner, rather than later. You will also need to call the senior lien holder, advise them of the situation, and ask them what you need to do to assume the senior loan. If you talk to the lender beforehand, the transition of the property will probably be a much smoother process.

Let's look at examples of when it's a good time to move forward with foreclosure.

Suppose the borrower is two payments behind. If your loan is the first mortgage, and you have talked to the borrower without any cooperation, then you need not waste any more time. File the foreclosure. On the other hand, if there is a lot of equity and it looks like the borrower is going to bring his loan current, or, is in the process of refinancing, give him more time.

If yours is a second mortgage, however, and the borrower is behind on your Note, then your first step is to call the first mortgage lender to see if the borrower is delinquent with them. If he is behind with the first loan, you need to file your foreclosure as fast as you can, so you are in the driver's seat. You want your foreclosure to go to the trustee sale before the senior lien holder's and at this time, you should advance the delinquent payments to the senior lien holder. If the senior lien holder files a foreclosure, then there is an additional cost. If you do end up with the property, you will save that expense.

Having said that, every situation is different and every investor is different. We all have our own personalities and our own unique ever-changing financial situation. There is no right or wrong solution. Nothing is set in stone. I'm giving you scenarios so you know them and can figure out how to forge ahead, using your own creative intuition. You will need to decide what is right for you, at any given time.

When you are actually to the point of filing the foreclosure, you must take copies of the Note and the Deed to the Title or Foreclosure Company. They will do the rest. Most Foreclosure Companies charge about $500 up front, to handle the process. That cost is passed on to the borrower.

Once the Title Company files a notice of default, it's advisable for you to let the first mortgage lender know, so they don't file their foreclosure on any future delinquency. If the borrower doesn't keep them current, you may, or may not, decide to make those payments right away. It's up to you now, because, you're in the driver's seat. If the property goes to sale, it's going on your deed, and, as the junior Trust Deed holder, you have the same right as the borrower to re-instate the senior lien, or, to make the payments on it.

The borrower has three months from the date that the notice of default is recorded, to bring the loan current and pay all foreclosure fees, including any advance payments you made to the senior lender. The first mortgage, and the insurance and property taxes, have to be current, as well. If the borrower is unable to cure the default, the foreclosure process moves into what is called the publication period. The trustee is required, by law, to publish a notice of sale at least twenty-one days before the sell date, but not before the three-month period is over.

The trustee, again, notifies all the parties concerned of the impending sale. The trustee's notice of the impending foreclosure sale is published once a week, for three successive weeks, in a local newspaper with general circulation. Even during the publication period, the borrower has the right to reinstate the loan, up until five business days before the auction. After that time, it is then up to the lender whether or not they let the borrower to reinstate the loan. Otherwise, the loan has to be paid off, in order to cure the default.

Another option, rarely exercised, is the judicial foreclosure, wherein, a lender files an action in Superior Court. Only in cases of fraud, where the Note was not a purchased money Note, or, the security is almost zero, would a lender resort to the judicial method of foreclosure.

Once you file foreclosure, do not communicate with the borrower and don't accept any payments. If you accept a payment, you void the foreclosure. If the borrower wants to cure the default, he needs to go through the foreclosure company. He owes them fees, and they will have to legally cancel the foreclosure notice. The foreclosure company handles all of the legalities and paperwork: the filing of the notice of default, posting of the notice of default, publication of the notice of default, the trustee's sale guarantee, and the posting of the notice of trustees' sale at the front door of the property. They'll send copies of notice of default to all the parties concerned, within ten and thirty days of filing the notice of default. The foreclosure company will also conduct the auction, or, have it conducted by a professional auction company.

Even though the foreclosure company is doing all the work, you, as an investor, should follow it very closely, because they're handling hundreds of foreclosures. The whole process is one of teamwork. With you directly involved, things will move along smoother. It will be to your advantage to remind the foreclosure company, two weeks before the three-month period is over, that they will need to prepare and schedule the publication of the trustee sale notice. Since the borrower sometimes needs just one extra day or, one extra week to either get a temporary restraining order (TRO) or file bankruptcy, time is very crucial.

The trustee or the lender can postpone a trustee sale three times. The borrower is allowed one postponement for one business day, in order to raise cash to redeem the property. If there are three postponements, there should be a good reason for it, otherwise, you may have to republish again. Other postponements can be caused by a borrower filing bankruptcy or by court order. When someone's about to lose his or her house, he's going to do anything possible to save it.

Even other parties, with equitable interest in the property, can get a court to issue a temporary restraining order to postpone a trustee sale. If you receive a TRO, read it very carefully, to see the basis for it, and make sure your attorney acts on it fast. Once a foreclosure is filed, the borrower not only gets letters from other lenders and investors, but also from attorneys. Some attorneys want to help the borrower file bankruptcy, while others want to go through the loan documents with a microscope to find any violations or improprieties. That can be cause for aggravation; how big or small depends on the mistakes made in the loan transaction. This is another reason why the loan documents have to be in complete compliance.

There have been cases where mortgage companies did not comply with the law. Depending on how serious the violations were, and, if it ends up in the court, the Judge has the power to reduce the loan amount, alter the terms of the Note, and waive the interest totally, or, even to expunge the loan. In some cases, where the borrower is a senior citizen, and it was apparent that the borrower could not make the payments, the loan did not make sense and excessive fees were charged, there can even be criminal consequences.

The foreclosure sale is held on the auction date, either in front of the courthouse, or, at another designated public place. The trustee reads the trustee sale notice, which is called "crying the sale." He then announces the lender's opening bid.

Other bids are taken from people who have pre-qualified with the trustee. The buyer with the highest bid gets the property.

All bids, except a lender's bid, are accepted in the form of cash or cashier's check, only.

If it's the first mortgage foreclosing and the bid is over the minimum amount, the money left over will be applied to junior lien holders, in order of their priority, first. Any surplus will then be given to the borrower. If there's no money over the minimum bid and there's a second mortgage, that mortgage will be wiped out. The junior lien holder can no longer look to the property as security. It's called "sold out." If the junior lien holder is foreclosing and ends up with the property, as stated earlier, he has the right to assume all senior liens. Remember, when you make a Trust Deed loan your ability to collect is limited to the equity in the subject property. You cannot go after the borrower for any deficiency.

If you, as an investor, end up with the property, then begins the process of taking possession of the property. If the property is occupied, the investor will have to file an *unlawful detainer* lawsuit to evict the borrower. If it is a rental, then the lease, or, month to month agreement, is terminated, unless a lease is recorded before your deed. Always get copy of the rental agreement whenever you make a loan on non-owner property. It is a good idea to contact the tenants before the sale, and get their names, along with a copy of their rental agreement, if you don't already have one. Once you get the title to the property, you can evict them, unless you want them to stay under the existing terms, or, new lease terms.

There are investors out there who have been investing money in Trust Deeds for forty plus years, and who have gone through many foreclosures without a problem. On the other hand, I know investors whose very first Trust Deed Investment went into a long, convoluted foreclosure. Fortunately, they kept at it and twenty years later, they're still making good money in the Trust Deed Investments.

BANKRUPTCY

FOR EVERY TRUST DEED INVESTOR, the fear of a borrower going into bankruptcy looms large. It's a legitimate concern. That's why it's important to know who you're loaning money to. Do a good, thorough job while originating a Trust Deed and you'll be less likely to have a borrower filing bankruptcy. Trust deed investment is very safe if you, or, your Mortgage Broker, know what you're doing.

Nobody can predict the future. For even a seasoned bank loan underwriter, the only concern is to make sure it's a good loan at the time of origination. It may very well be the safest loan possible on paper, at that time, yet, within months, the borrower may file bankruptcy for any number of unforeseen reasons. That's no reflection on the loan underwriter. Yet, the fact remains, bankruptcy can happen. As an investor, if you understand the bankruptcy procedure, then you won't be afraid of it. First, never make a loan to someone who appears to potentially be ready to file bankruptcy. At the same time, you should not overlook a great opportunity to invest in Trust Deeds simply because a homeowner could file bankruptcy.

Briefly, there are two kinds of bankruptcies. One kind is for the purpose of reorganization, and the other is for the purpose of liquidating the debtor's assets.

The first kind of bankruptcy has two chapters: Chapter Thirteen, which is for individuals, and Chapter Eleven, which is for corporations, partnerships, or individuals who owe substantial debts and don't qualify for Chapter Thirteen.

Liquidation bankruptcy is known as Chapter Seven, or, as a straight bankruptcy. Both businesses and individuals can file straight bankruptcy. Assuming there's equity in excess of the allowed homestead exemption ($50,000 for single, $75,000 for married and $150,000 for seniors) in the house, a straight bankruptcy is desirable for an investor, since everything, including the house, may be liquidated to pay off the debts.

Once a borrower files bankruptcy, everything comes screeching to a halt. The foreclosure action is stayed. The notice of default, filed before the bankruptcy filing, is still valid, but, stayed. Once the stay is lifted, you generally do not need to file a new notice of default.

A Chapter Seven or Chapter Eleven bankruptcy generally only applies to actions against the debtor. It does not protect a co-signor or a guarantor, unless they filed for bankruptcy, also.

In a Chapter Thirteen filing, co-debtors may also be protected. The bankruptcy stay does not stop you from dealing with senior or junior lien holders and bringing them current. Interestingly enough, if a junior lien holder files bankruptcy, it will stop the senior lien holder from foreclosing. The first thing you will need to do is find a competent bankruptcy attorney, preferably in the same city and county where the property is located. They will be able to counsel you about the situation and your legal options. A listing of certified bankruptcy specialists for the State of California can be found online, from the California Bar Association web site. Other states may also have similar listings. If not, call your state bar association for help in finding an attorney.

Once you've retained a bankruptcy attorney, keep in close contact. Learn the ropes by taking on some of the work and research. Don't leave everything to your attorney.

Here are some of the things you should know, and do, in this situation:

1. How far behind is the borrower on the first mortgage? This is crucial to know if yours is a second mortgage.

2. Be prepared to bring the senior loan(s) and any delinquent taxes current, by advancing the delinquent payments. Check with your attorney as to the best time to do so.

3. File a *proof of claim* right away, even though you are a secured lender, and by law, you may not have to. If the house has minimal or no equity, or, if the debtor fails to make any post-petition payments, have your attorney file a petition to the court to lift the stay. Petitions to lift the stay are considered on a priority basis and may be heard within thirty days. Your attorney will, of course, give you the best advice for your particular case.

4. Check the value that the debtor places on the home in his or her schedules. If you believe this value to be unrealistic, then you may want to, at least, run a comp check for valuation and, if your attorney so advises, order a new appraisal from a professional appraiser — preferably a new or different one, who hasn't evaluated the property before. There are appraisers who specialize in doing appraisals for bankruptcies, but, it really doesn't matter, as long as they're certified.

If the new appraisal shows little or no equity in the property, your petition for relief of stay will show to the court that a delay would only cost the lenders their investment, without helping the borrower.

Go to court with proper and complete documentation, including the recent appraisal, to support your claims. You should have the dollar amount the borrower owes on the property written down to the penny, including:

- first mortgage balance
- delinquent first mortgage payments
- first mortgage foreclosure fees
- attorney fees
- late charges
- *your* delinquent payments
- payments you advanced to the first mortgage holder and the interest thereon
- delinquent taxes
- delinquent fire insurance premium
- homeowner association fees, if applicable

If your case is strong and presented effectively, you should have little problem getting the stay lifted. It may not happen right then and there, but, it will happen soon. More often than not, the Judge may grant you the relief from stay, but, at the same time, give the borrower sixty to ninety days to sell the property.

In case your request for a relief from stay is not granted, then your bankruptcy attorney has other strategies. If the borrower wants time to refinance or sell the property, then your attorney can get a stipulation that will provide a specific timeline for this to happen. If they do not refinance or sell within the time allotted, the stay will be automatically lifted. Speaking of stipulations, even though the Note and Trust Deed give you the right to collect attorney and foreclosure fees, the trustee may not give them to you, unless ordered by the Judge, specifically. Also, if the borrower in bankruptcy isn't keeping the property in good, normal condition, your attorney needs to bring it to the courts attention. (Take some pictures for documentation.)

If the loan is secured by an investment property, your Trust Deed gives you the power to ask the court to direct the debtor to turn over the rental payments to you.

If you've filed a notice of default before the borrower filed bankruptcy, then you do not need to file again after the stay is lifted. If you were already into the publication period, you don't have to start the twenty-one day cycle over again. Although, you will want to publish the new sale date, to ensure a good turn out of investors interested in the property.

As mentioned in the chapter on foreclosure, once the attorneys get involved, every loan document will be combed through with a critical eye. The bankruptcy court has limited power to alter the terms of the loan. You're entitled to receive payments on your loan, but, the Judge can grant the debtor some time to make good on any missed payments. In cases where there's absolutely no equity to cover your property, the court may declare your claim to be similar to that of an unsecured creditor. This would only happen if you totally misjudged the value of the property, or, if you simply failed to take any action over the extended period that the debtor made no payments.

It's important to reiterate that where there is substantial equity in a property, the interests of everyone involved are better served if the debtor is given some time to cure any defaults to the lender, or, to sell or refinance the property.

CHAPTER 9

IRA/KEOGH INVESTMENTS

IF YOU HAVE MORE THAN $20,000 in your IRA plan, it's time to get smart and take control of your investments. Convert it into a self-directed IRA and choose where you would like to invest your money. Most people don't know the tremendous advantage of a self-directed IRA. In fact, most people don't even know that they can invest their IRA anywhere they want, or, transfer it from one account to another. As long as you don't take any money out, there's no problem in moving your IRA around. There are a few financial firms who, for a nominal fee, can administer your self-directed IRA plan, and get you a much higher return rate than you're getting from your bank.

The same rules apply to KEOGH. If you're self-employed, you can set aside a part of your income each year in a KEOGH plan, which is most likely locked into a low interest rate plan. Get out of it. Convert it into a self-directed KEOGH plan, which gives you the flexibility of moving it around to different investments, in order to get maximum yield.

Let's say, for instance, that right now you are depositing $500 a month into your KEOGH plan at an interest rate of 7%. Twenty years from now, you'll have accumulated $261,982.69. But, if you would have invested the same money in Trust Deeds at a 15% annual rate of return, in twenty years you would have accumulated $757,977.48.

CHAPTER 10

REPORTING INTEREST INCOME

THE INTEREST INCOME FROM YOUR Trust Deed Investment is treated like ordinary income. If you buy a Trust Deed at a discount, you can amortize the discount over the term of the Note. If you buy a discounted Note, and it goes into default, with the end result of you owning the property after the trustee's sale, you may have to pay taxes on the full amount of the Note. If, however, you think that there will be no other bidders at the trustee sale, or, you really don't want to own the property, you may consider opening the bid at the discounted value of the Trust Deed Note, instead of the face amount. Consult your attorney and accountant.

Late charges and prepayment penalties are also considered ordinary income. If you charged any loan fees or any points, you have to report them in the same year you collected them.

CHAPTER 11

AB489 – PREDATORY LENDING "THE 900LB GORILLA"

A WORD ON CALIFORNIA FINANCIAL CODE 4970

MAKING MONEY IS ONE THING. Keeping it - is another. All of us know that real estate is a good investment and yet, we all know someone who's lost money in real estate. Most people learn in life by their own mistakes. Wise people learn from other people's mistakes. Behind every success story, there's a lot of planning, hard work, perseverance, patience, and knowledge about the rules and laws, but, above all, there is instinct and luck.

As we've discussed, there is always some risk in Trust Deed Investments, just as there is risk in any investment that gives you a decent return. But, there's a new nine-hundred pound gorilla, in the form of a new law: California Financial Code 4970, also known as AB489 or The Predatory Lending Law. It's an expansion of the Home Ownership

Equity Protection Act of 1994 (HOEPA). According to "Stolen Wealth: Inequities in California's Sub-prime Mortgage Market," produced by the California Reinvestment Committee, thirty-six percent of the sub-prime loans surveyed in California were deemed predatory. This brings us to one specific law you must understand if you're going to invest in Trust Deeds. If you don't understand and abide by this law, you could wind up in a heap of trouble.

The anti-predatory lending law, or AB489, is triggered when a loan is less than the Fannie Mae conforming loan limit (at the time this book was written the limit was $417,000 – this amount increases periodically), and the annual percentage rate (APR), exceeds by eight percentage points, the yield on Treasury securities with comparable periods of maturity on the 15th day of the month immediately preceding the month in which the loan was originated. Or, the total points and fees paid by the borrower exceed six percent of the loan amount. The total fees referred to here are the fees that go into the broker's or the lender's pocket. Escrow fees are also included in total fees. Title insurance, appraisal, notary, flood certification, and tax service fees are not included.

Excluded from AB489 are:
- Non-owner occupied properties
- Equity lines of credit
- Purchase money loans
- First lien Reverse Mortgages

Since laws are in a constant state of change, and subject to interpretation, especially new ones that have never been tested in a court of law, check with your attorney on the above exclusions and about everything else in this book.

Although it's true that there are some Mortgage Lenders and Brokers who are not that knowledgeable, or, just don't care as long as they can close the deal, there are also more lawyers these days taking advantage of brokers not following the procedures and laws to the letter, and suing them. The more Mortgage Brokers and Lenders are sued, the more they are going to tighten their lending policies. Eventually, it will become more difficult for borrowers, who are in trouble financially and are facing foreclosure, to borrow money.

It's not that the lender or a broker cannot make a loan that falls under AB489. They can, but, they need to give additional disclosures to the borrower and the borrower has to meet certain conditions. The loan is stated income, but, the Broker must reasonably believe that borrowers can make the payments. Also, the borrower will have to review and sign all the disclosures, and then, wait for three days before the actual loan documents can be signed. And then, the rescission period kicks in. There is also a specific verbiage that goes in the Promissory Note: "If you obtain this loan, the lender will have a mortgage on your home. You could lose your home, and any money you have put into it, if you do not meet your obligations under the loan." The borrower also has to get a letter from an attorney or a Certified Public Accountant (CPA), stating that it's not detrimental for them to take this loan.

AB489 prohibits repeated refinancing by the same lender. The rules now limit a creditor from refinancing loans within a year, unless the creditor can demonstrate that refinancing is in the "borrower's interest." Assignees, holding or servicing a HOEPA loan, are covered by this rule, as if they were the original creditors.

AB489 also places responsibility for picking the best loan for the borrower on the shoulders of brokers. If the borrower qualified for a regular conventional or bank loan, and the broker put the borrower into another loan with terms that were not as favorable, the broker is at risk of violating AB489.

AB489 allows no prepayment penalty after three years, and the broker must offer the borrower a loan product without the pre-payment penalty. The debt ratio cannot be more than 50% on a covered loan. An investor is also prohibited from collecting more than two months prepaid interest at the time of origination of the loan. No advance payments are allowed. There cannot be a balloon payment for the first five years, unless it's a construction or bridge loan. Any loan with a term of less than five years has to be fully amortized. The investor cannot collect interest on the principal for a period of more than one day prior to recording the Deed of Trust. The interest rate cannot be increased upon filing foreclosure, and any pre-payment will have to be waived.

Also, AB489 prohibits making loans that the borrower will be unable to repay. If a borrower is over sixty-five, and it can be proven that the mortgage broker was fully aware that this borrower could not make the payment, and will lose the house, the broker can be criminally charged.

AB489 prohibits credit insurance financing. Credit insurance often forces borrowers to pay interest on already high insurance premiums; something the Consumer Federation of America has called "the worst insurance rip-off" in the nation.

Sub-prime loans are more costly, because they are considered to be more risky. As a result, investors want higher yields. This makes sense. The problem comes when a broker or lender abuses it, and charges exorbitant rates and fees. The irony is that borrowers, who actually need a lower rate and lower payment, end up paying a higher rate with a higher payment. It's a good thing this law does not cover purchase loans; otherwise, some borrowers would definitely not be able to fulfill the American dream of homeownership.

Unfortunately, AB489 actually limits access to the equity in one's own property. There are many cases where people get laid off or have a death in the family of someone who contributes an income, and they need to borrow against the equity of their home until they get back on their feet. If one follows AB489 to the letter, these homeowners will not be able to borrow money and may end up losing their home. Equity-based borrowing has helped a large section of the community, at one point or another. AB489 is a tough law. Some people, who have benefited from a bailout loan before, would now not be able to get one because of AB489. Consequently, they'll lose all of the equity in their home, unless, they move fast and sell, to save whatever equity they can. The problem is when your home is in foreclosure, buyers with financing low ball you, and people with cash simply wait until the home goes to auction.

If you are going to invest in Trust Deeds, make sure any mortgage company you are working with, that is originating Hard Money Loans, is following the law to a "T." After all, it is your money that is on the line. Make sure that the total fees that are going into the broker's pocket, along with the escrow fee, are no more than 6% of the total loan amount, if it is a covered loan. Also, make sure that the APR does not exceed, by eight percentage points, the yield on treasury securities with comparable periods of maturity on the 15th day of the month immediately preceding the month in which the application for extension of credit is received by the creditor.

Just to reiterate, the above restrictions apply only on covered loans.

CHAPTER 12
TRUST DEED FORMS AND FACTS

THE PRELIMINARY TITLE REPORT (PRELIM)

ALL HOME LOANS SHOULD BE insured by a Title Company. When a borrower applies for a home loan, whether it is a purchase, refinance, or an equity loan, the lender opens an escrow and title search with a Title Company. The Title Company searches the county records and provides the lender or Mortgage Broker with a report which contains the following information:

1. The date of the preliminary title report
2. The name(s) of the owner(s) or vestee(s)
3. A legal description, the street address of the property and the assessor's parcel number
4. Any mortgage(s) or deed(s) on the property
5. The original loan amount of the senior lien in the prelim.
6. The names and addresses of the owner(s) or the beneficiary(s) of the existing mortgages(s)

7. Requests for notices concerning status of the liens, notices of default, and notices of trustee's sale

8. Notice of a lawsuit or bankruptcy affecting the property

9. Property taxes — whether paid or delinquent

10. Assessor's plat map, which illustrates the configuration, dimensions, and general location of the property

11. Any unpaid assessments or association dues

12. Any unpaid judgments or involuntary liens

13. A notice of default or bankruptcy, if one exists

14. Any divorce settlement or suit pending

Carefully scrutinize the Title Report to make sure it is current and not more than fifteen days old. What you see here is what you get. This is the Title Company's guarantee that the borrower is the legal owner of the subject property. If, at a later date, you find that the borrower was not the legal owner of the property, or, had no right to borrow on the subject property, the Title Insurance will have to pay you off. The Title Report also guarantees that the voluntary and involuntary liens on the property, as listed in the Prelim in specific order, are the only liens on the subject property. Later, if more liens show up, which the Title Company missed, your title insurance will protect you and cover any incurred losses. Title Companies are multi billion dollar corporations and they know what they are doing. There isn't one situation which they haven't already experienced. They provide great protection, for a relatively small premium which is paid by the borrower.

If there are things on the Title Report that are not supposed to be there, the Title Company can issue you a corrected and updated Preliminary Title Report. If you are funding the loan directly, make sure that the Title Company follows your instructions. For example, if the borrower already has a first and a second mortgage, and you're supposed to be giving the borrower a new second mortgage, then the Title Company should be instructed to pay-off the existing second Trust Deed. That way, your new loan will be in the second position. If the taxes are delinquent, the Title Company should bring the taxes current from the loan proceeds, and your title insurance policy reflects that.

All judgments should also be paid off from the loan proceeds in escrow and deleted from the Title Report. Such deletions will be shown only in your title insurance policy, which the Title Company mails to the lender within 30 days from the closing of the loan transaction. Make sure that the borrower's name is the same on the Preliminary Title Report, the Note, and the Deed. Also check that the property address and Assessor's Parcel Number (APN) are correct, and match your Deed of Trust.

Each Title Company has its own format for the Preliminary Title Report, but, the information provided will always be the same.

ALL ABOUT NOTES

A NOTE IS NOTHING MORE than an "I OWE YOU". Even the dollar bill in your wallet is legally a Note. Read it. It says so, right on the top of the bill: "FEDERAL RESERVE NOTE".

A note specifies:

1. The amount of the loan (the principal)

2. The interest rate (interest)

3. The amount of each payment (payment or debt service)

4. The number of payments (terms of the loan)

5. When the loan is to be paid-off (due date)

6. Provision for penalties if the borrower is late on his payments (late charge) or decides to pay-off the loan before the due date (prepayment penalty)

Notes can be secured or unsecured. Your credit cards and personal loans are all unsecured Notes, and your auto loan is a secured Note. If you don't make payments, as stated in the terms of your Note, the bank can repossess your automobile. In the case of unsecured Notes, the bank first has to sue, get a judgment, and then, collect on that judgment.

In some States, which are called the Mortgage States, Mortgage Notes are similar with other Notes in such that they do not have the same inherent power of a Trust Deed, to foreclose without going through the judicial system. In Mortgage States, the Mortgage holder has to go through the court to foreclose. Not only that, after the property is repossessed, the borrower still has a year to redeem the property. States that have Trust Deeds with inherent power to foreclose are good for investors, as well as for the borrowers, because more money is available to invest in real estate and Trust Deeds.

Fortunately for us, we are not dealing with unsecured Notes. We are dealing with Notes secured and backed by the best security one can possibly offer: one's home. When a real estate Note is secured by a Deed of Trust, that gives the trustee the power to foreclose in case of default; nothing can beat the desirability of owning that Note.

TRUST DEED

WHAT MAKES THE TRUST DEED such an attractive tool for investors? It's because the Trust Deed is a legal document that exercises certain powers. Basically, a Trust Deed states that the borrower (the trustor) transfers the property, in *trust*, to an independent third party (the trustee), who holds conditional title on behalf of the lender or investor (the beneficiary). The Trustee can then:

1. Re-convey the deed once the loan is paid off; and or
2. Sell the property should there be default (foreclosure).

Foreclosure is the process of selling the property to a third-party bidder or, in the absence of a sufficient third-party bid, acquiring title to the property. The foreclosure sale, in most cases, satisfies the debt, but not always. This will depend upon the method and handling of the delinquency or foreclosure, the quality of the Note, the desirability and value of the property, the loan to value ratio, and how much equity cushion you have. All of these factors will determine whether or not you will be able to recover your entire investment.

For example, if a third party bids at a trustee's sale, for an amount equal to, or greater than, the amount that you're owed, (including fees, costs, and expenses of the foreclosure), your investment would be fully paid. On the other hand, if you bid the full amount that is owed you, (including all foreclosure fees, costs, and expenses), and there are no third-party bids, you will then own the property. You can either keep the property for long term investment or sell it.

There's a short form Trust Deed and a regular FNMA Trust Deed. The short form Trust Deed consists of only the front page of the regular Trust Deed. It does away with the rest of the pages. They're already recorded with the County Recorder's office and are referred to as the fictitious Trust Deed.

It's the Deed of Trust recorded against the title of the borrower's subject property that really secures your investment. The Note itself is not a security instrument. It's just a promise to pay. However, when secured by a recorded Trust Deed, the Note becomes very powerful.

In a Trust Deed Note, the borrower allows the lender or investor to put a voluntary lien on the borrower's property. When you bought the house and the bank made a loan to you, you signed a Note and a Deed of Trust. The bank actually made a Trust Deed Investment. Unless the Trust Deed is recorded with the County Recorder's office in the county where the property is located, it's unsecured. Recording of a Trust Deed gives a constructive notice to the public of the lien on the property.

Not only does a Trust Deed have to be recorded, but, the timing is crucial, as well.

Suppose Bob owns a home. He needs some fast cash and he asks his friend Bill for a short-term loan of $20,000. To make Bill comfortable, Borrower Bob signs a ninety-day straight Note and a Deed of Trust for 20,000. Bill loans Bob $20,000 for ninety days. However, Bill is too trusting and he does not get the Deed recorded. Since the deed is not recorded, no one, except Bob and Bill, know that there is supposed to be a $20,000 lien against Bob's property.

Guess what? Borrower Bob's house burns down the next week, and the insurance company refuses to pay Bill $20,000 because his deed was not recorded.

What if Borrower Bob gets involved in litigation and the plaintiff slaps a *lis pendense* on Bob's property? The *lis pendense* takes precedence over Bill's Deed of Trust because it was never recorded. Even if Bill records his deed now, it may be too late. The same would be true if the IRS or a collection agency recorded a lien before Investor Bill recorded his deed.

A Note secured by an unrecorded Deed of Trust is an unsecured Note. It is very important to record a deed first, before handing the money over to a borrower. In any event, you should always consider using a Title Company for these transactions. It'll save you lot of potential headaches down the road.

REQUEST FOR COPY OF NOTICE OF DEFAULT

ANYTIME YOU MAKE A SECOND or junior mortgage, you want to make sure that the Title Company records a request for copy of Notice of Default. This will ensure that if the senior lender forecloses, they will have to notify you within ten days of that foreclosure being recorded. That gives you a head start, to cure the default and file your own foreclosure.

REQUEST FOR NOTICE OF DELINQUENCY

THE REQUEST FOR COPY OF Notice of Default is very useful, although, it does have a small shortfall. Some lenders, especially lenders with the Federal Housing Administration Loans (FHA), may let the borrower fall behind in his payments for almost a year, before they actually file a Notice of Default. These lenders will keep working with the borrower, in an attempt to assist them in catching up on delinquent payments.

Soon the borrower is not just two, but, many payments behind, before the lender files foreclosure and sends you a copy of the Notice of Default. You, as a second lien holder, now have to shell out thousands of dollars to bring the senior lien holder current, and then, turn around and file your own foreclosure. You, of course, wish the lender would have foreclosed when the borrower was only two payments behind, or, at least, informed you. You could have brought their loan current when it was just two months or so behind, instead of many months behind.

Fortunately, there's way to solve this problem. The way around it is by recording a request for notice of delinquency, and mailing a copy of the recorded request, along with a $40 fee, to the senior lien holder. If you do this, then the senior lien holder is obligated by law to inform you of the delinquency during the first four months.

In addition, the request for notice of delinquency also gives you clout with the senior lender. If the borrower is more than thirty days past due on his payment to you, you can pick up the phone and check on the status of the senior loan. It's possible that the borrower will keep on making payments to you, but, not to the senior lender.

This request for notice of delinquency has a life of five years. Refer to Section 2924e of the Civil Code on Foreclosure, for information on getting an extension.

With this notice requested, you, as an investor or, your mortgage company, have done a tremendous job. As a smart Trust Deed investor or a Mortgage Broker, you don't want to ignore this powerful tool. Make full use of it.

FIRE INSURANCE LOSS PAYEE

A TRUST DEED LOAN SHOULD never be funded until you have "the insurance loss payee" from the homeowner's fire insurance company. It names the investor as a first or second mortgage lender, or, a beneficiary loss payee, in the case of a loss or damage to the property. The property should have enough coverage for both the first and the second mortgage, should the house burn down. Most insurance policies have a replacement cost clause, which is accepted by almost all lenders, as sufficient insurance coverage to cover the loan in case of fire damage. It is a good idea, however, to have a specific dollar amount that covers all the liens on the property. The borrower pays for any cost incurred, by increasing the insurance coverage.

BALLOON PAYMENT NOTICE

ALL LOANS WITH BALLOON PAYMENTS should have a notice of the same to the borrower. The borrower signs it, at the time he signs all other loan documents. This notice lets the borrower know, in clear and explicit terms, that the loan has a balloon payment clause. It also requires the holder of the Note (you as the investor), to give written notice to the trustor, or his successor in interest, of the prescribed information, in at least ninety days, and not more than one hundred fifty days, before any balloon payment is due. Simply put, if you are the Note holder on a loan with a balloon payment, you need to notify the borrower by certified and regular mail, within at least ninety days, but, not more than, one hundred fifty days, before any balloon payment is due. The notification should clearly state the date on which the balloon payment is due.

APPRAISAL

IF YOU'RE IN THE BUSINESS of buying Trust Deeds, you'll need to make sure you have appraisals on all of the properties you are dealing with. You can do the appraisal yourself, but, if you're selling the Trust Deed, it's definitely better to have an independent appraiser do the work. It's not the format of the appraisal that's so important, but, the honesty and accuracy.

In some cases, where the LTV is below 50% and you can get independent information about the property, a plain fact sheet, with the pertinent information on the age of the property, square footage, and number of bedrooms and baths, along with at least three comparable sales of like properties in the immediate neighborhood within last six months, is all that's necessary. Most investors, who invest in local properties and buy Trust Deeds from Mortgage Brokers, do their own drive-by inspection of the property, and call a few brokers who have listings in that neighborhood to verify value.

Compliance Agreement

Most professional Mortgage Brokers use a compliance agreement form. The borrower signs the form, which states that if there are any mistakes made during the loan transaction, including mistakes in the documentation, the borrower will comply and co-operate to correct such mistakes. It's a very useful tool. There have been times when the borrower's name has been miss-spelled or the property address has been missing on the Deed of Trust and so on. In such cases, the borrower is obligated to come back to the Title Company and help correct whatever needs to be done.

3-DAY RESCISSION NOTICE

ON ALL OWNER-OCCUPIED PROPERTY REFINANCES and equity loans, the lender is required to give the borrower a three day right of rescission. Simply stated, after the borrower signs all the loan documents, the borrower has three days to think it over. He can, without any obligation or penalty, cancel the loan within those three working days after signing, if he doesn't like the loan. Saturday is considered a working day.

LENDER'S INSTRUCTIONS

ONCE YOU OR THE MORTGAGE Broker decides to fund a Trust Deed loan, the lender's instructions will be issued to the Title Company. The format does not matter. The idea is to instruct the Title Company of what you would like to be done. In most cases, the investor lets the mortgage company handle it. When you fund the loan, you want to make sure that the following items are correct; your loan is in the right position (first or second), the property taxes are current, and all other liens that are supposed to be paid-off, are paid. You can verify this by requesting a copy of the estimated HUD1 statement, which spells out the transaction. You can also give your own instructions, in addition to the mortgage company's instructions.

<u>**Here are sample instructions to the Title Company:**</u>

To:

ABC TITLE COMPANY

123 B Street

Any City, CA 91234

Attention:_____Amount of Loan:_____

Escrow No.:_____Borrowers Name:_____

Lender:_____

Dear Escrow officer:

In regards to the above escrow, I/We will be funding this loan directly. Please provide me with a funding package as soon as the borrower signs the loan documents. I will need the following:

- Original and a certified copy of the NOTE
- Certified copy of the Deed of Trust
- Certified copy of Request for Notice of Default and a copy of Request for Notice of Delinquency (if you are doing a second mortgage)
- Copy of estimated settlement sheet (HUD1)
- Insurance Loss Payee with coverage paid up to a year. The fire insurance policy to have replacement cost clause or increase coverage to $_____.

Upon notice that you are in a position to record this transaction, you may request loan funds in the amount of $_____, which you are authorized to disburse when you can issue your CLTA lender's title insurance policy on the property described in your above named numbered escrow, vested of record in our borrower, and insuring ____(your name)_____as beneficiary, subject only to items No._____of your preliminary title report dated_____, and when you hold for our account the above listed documents signed by borrowers.

Real estate and any other supplemental taxes, along with first mortgage (if you are funding a second mortgage loan) are to be paid current.

This loan is subject to items: of your Prelim dated:

Pay-off and delete items:

You are to collect all fees and charges from the borrowers. Please notify us when you have recorded our deed of trust and provide us with a copy of the recorded Deed of Trust or serial number, along with your final closing statement.

                                                            Date:_____

_____

Investor or Mortgage Company

CONCLUSION

So, why is any of this information on Trust Deed investing important? As we began this guide, we covered the possibilities first, and it comes back to this: most of us want our retirement years to be, at the very least, comfortable and secure. No one who works most of their adult life should be sitting around at seventy years old, worrying, because their savings are dwindling quickly. You get up every morning, you work hard, and you look after your family. You deserve some peace of mind in your golden years.

As much as you deserve that peace of mind, no one is going to hand it to you. You are going to have to work for it, and by work for it, I mean: Make a plan and act on it; then, stick to it.

Let's recap the steps:

You're going to go open a savings account, if you haven't already done so, and you're going to put 10% of your earnings into that account on each payday - faithfully. Maybe this book will motivate you to get more involved at your workplace, give 110% of yourself, and get a big fat raise. Or, maybe you won't be able to dine out as often as you'd like.

You may have to work at cutting corners, but, you will wake up, one day soon, and realize that you have doubled your savings.

Next, you're going to take those savings, find a reliable Mortgage Broker and invest in Trust Deeds. You're going to take all of this how-to information and really make your money work for you. No longer will you be letting your money work for others. You're going to take control and make your own investment decisions. It's that simple.

Trust Deeds are safe, Trust Deeds are secure, and you can easily get returns in the 10 to 18% range. Most important, you have control over your investment. Not every transaction will go perfectly, but most will. Even the ones that don't initially go well, will eventually end up in your favor, as long as you follow all of the information in this book and play by the rules laid out here. It might take a little work and a little time, but you can do it. No one is promising overnight success; it takes some effort to become successful in anything, including Trust Deed Investments. But, think about it. With the information you're holding in your hands — in this book – you can actually retire a millionaire!

It all starts with you today – right here, right now.

Appendix

LENDER/PURCHASER DISCLOSURE STATEMENT

IN CALIFORNIA, A MORTGAGE BROKER is reguired by law to provide the investor with the form 851A, if it is a new loan origination and form 851B, if it is sale of an existing Note. A sample of the form is included herewith. Basically, the form provides you with every bit of detail and answer almost all of your questions about the Note. The form is self-explanatory, but, nevertheless, I am going to list few things it covers:

1. Is this a multi-lender transaction?
2. Is there more than one property securing the Note?
3. Amount of the new loan
4. What is the market value of the property?
5. Total amount of loans senior to the new loan (Obviously this will happen only if you are doing a second or a third mortgage)
6. Total amount of loans anticipated or expected to be junior to this new loan (This will happen if there is going to be a

subordination or a new second or a junior mortgage going behind your loan)

7. Protective Equity (Market value minus the new loan and any senior loans)

8. Total Loan to Value (LTV) or Combined Loan to Value (CLTV)

9. Name, address, and capacity of the mortgage broker originating the loan

10. Part 3 of the form gives details of the Note like loan amount, rate, term, etc.

11. Part 4 applies only to multi-lender transactions

12. Part 5 details the servicing agreement between you and the mortgage broker

13. Part 6 is all about the borrower, borrower's income, expenses, occupation.

14. Part 7 covers the subject property information like whether it is owner or non-owner occupied and annual property taxes and whether they are current

15. Part 8 gives you the property description including square footage. It gives you the appraiser's information; date of the appraisal and the appraised value. If there is more than one property, securing the loan, that will be covered here too.

16. Part 9 gives you all the information about what is owed on the property now, or, the senior lien and how the borrower has paid on it during the last 12 months. It also tells you if the borrower is delinquent right now and, if so, for how many months. Obviously, if the loan is going to remain, you want to make sure that it is brought current.

17. Part 10 summarizes what is going to remain as encumbrance on the property and tells you what the LTV or CLTV is.

STATE OF CALIFORNIA

DEPARTMENT OF REAL ESTATE
MORTGAGE LENDING

LENDER/PURCHASER DISCLOSURE STATEMENT
(Loan Origination)

RE 851A (Rev. 2/04)

DISCLOSURE STATEMENT SUMMARY

Note: If this is a multi-lender transaction and more than one property secures the loan, you should also refer to the attached Lender/Purchaser Disclosure Statement Multi-Property (Cross Collateralization) Addendum (RE 851D).

AMOUNT OF THIS LOAN *(SEE PART 3)*	MARKET VALUE OF PROPERTY (SEE PART 8)	TOTAL AMOUNT OF ENCUMBRANCES SENIOR TO THIS LOAN *(SEE PART 9)*
$	$	$
TOTAL AMOUNT OF ENCUMBRANCES ANTICIPATED OR EXPECTED TO BE JUNIOR TO THIS LOAN *(SEE PART 9)*	PROTECTIVE EQUITY (MARKET VALUE MINUS THIS LOAN AND TOTAL SENIOR ENCUMBRANCES)	TOTAL LOAN TO VALUE (SEE PART 10G)
$	$	%

PART 1 — BROKER INFORMATION

NAME OF BROKER	REAL ESTATE LICENSE ID#
BUSINESS ADDRESS	TELEPHONE NUMBER
NAME OF BROKERS REPRESENTATIVE	

PART 2 — BROKER CAPACITY IN TRANSACTION

THE BROKER IDENTIFIED IN PART 1 OF THIS STATEMENT IS ACTING IN THE FOLLOWING CAPACITY IN THIS TRANSACTION: (CHECK AS APPLIES)

☐ A. Agent in arranging a loan on behalf of another

☐ B. Principal as a borrower of funds from which broker will directly or indirectly benefit other than through the receipt of commissions, fees and costs and expenses as provided by law for services as an agent.

☐ C. Funding a portion of this loan. *(Multi-lender transactions are subject to Business and Professions Code Section 10238.)*

IF MORE THAN ONE CAPACITY HAS BEEN CHECKED, PROVIDE EXPLANATION HERE.

IF !B2HAS BEEN CHECKED, THE BROKER INTENDS TO USE FUNDS FROM THE LENDER/PURCHASER IN THIS TRANSACTION FOR:

PART 3 — TRANSACTION INFORMATION

(CHECK IF APPLICABLE)

☐ THERE IS MORE THAN ONE PROPERTY SECURING THE LOAN. IF MULTI-LENDER LOAN, YOU SHOULD ALSO REFER TO ATTACHED RE 851D.

TERM OF LOAN	PRIORITY OF THIS LOAN (1ST, 2ND, ETC.)	PRINCIPAL AMOUNT $	YOUR SHARE IF MULTI-LENDER TRANS. $
INTEREST RATE ___% ☐ VARIABLE ☐ FIXED	(CHECK ONE) ☐ AMORTIZED ☐ PARTIALLY AMORTIZED	☐ INTEREST ONLY	***THE TRUST DEED WILL BE RECORDED.***
PAYMENT FREQUENCY ☐ MONTHLY ☐ WEEKLY	APPROXIMATE PAYMENT DUE DATE	AMOUNT OF PAYMENT $	YOUR SHARE IF MULTI-LENDER TRANS. $
BALLOON PAYMENT ☐ YES ☐ NO	APPROX. BALLOON PAYMENT DUE DATE	AMOUNT OF BALLOON PAYMENT $	YOUR SHARE IF MULTI-LENDER TRANS. $

Balloon Payment. A balloon payment is any installment payment (usually the payment due at maturity) which is greater than twice the amount of the smallest installment payment under the terms of the promissory note or sales contract.

The borrower/vendee may have to obtain a new loan or sell the property to make the balloon payment. If the effort is not successful it may be necessary for the holder of the note/contract to foreclose on the property as a means of collecting the amount owed.

There are subordination provisions. .... ☐ Yes ☐ No
If YES, explain here or on an attachment.

PART 4	MULTI-LENDER TRANSACTIONS

NAME OF ESCROW HOLDER	ANTICIPATED CLOSING DATE

ADDRESS OF ESCROW HOLDER

ESTIMATED LENDER COSTS	ESTIMATED BORROWER COSTS.
	Broker will provide you a copy of the "mort-gage loan disclosure statement" given to the borrower or a separate itemization of borrower's costs.

$ _____

$ _____

$ _____

TOTAL $ _____   TOTAL $ _____

Servicing

You will be a joint beneficiary with others on this note and you should request a list of names and addresses of the beneficiaries as of the close of escrow from the broker or servicing agent. The beneficiary(ies) holding more than 50% interest in the note may govern the actions to be taken on behalf of all holders in the event of default or other matters. See Civil Code Section 2941.9.

Loan To Value

GENERALLY the aggregate principal amount of the notes or interests sold, together with the unpaid principal amount of any encumbrances upon the real property senior thereto, shall not exceed the following percentages of the current market value of the real property as determined in writing by the broker or qualified appraiser.

Single-family residence, owner-occupied 80%

Single-family residence, not owner-occupied 75%

Commercial and income-producing properties 65%

Single-family residentially zoned lot or parcel which has installed off-site improvements including drainage, curbs, gutters, sidewalks, paved roads, and utilities as mandated by the political subdivision having jurisdiction over the lot or parcel 65%

Land which has been zoned for (and if required, approved for subdivision as) commercial or Residential development 50%

Other real property 35%

The percentage amounts specified above may be exceeded when and to the extent that the broker determines that the encumbrance of the property in excess of these percentages is reasonable and prudent considering all relevant factors pertaining to the real property. However, in no event shall the aggregate principal amount of the notes or interests sold, together with the unpaid principal amount of any encumbrances upon the property senior thereto, exceed 80 percent of the current fair market value of improved real property or 50 percent of the current fair market value of unimproved real property, except in the case of a single-family residentially zoned lot or parcel as defined above, which shall not exceed 65% of current fair market value of that lot or parcel. A written statement shall be prepared by the broker that sets forth the material considerations and facts that the broker relies upon for his or her determination which shall be disclosed to the lender or note purchaser(s) and retained as a part of the broker's record of the transaction.

NOTE: If more than one property secures this loan, you should also refer to attached RE 851D.

PART 5 — SERVICING ARRANGEMENTS

If the loan is to be serviced by a real estate broker you must be notified within ten (10) days if the broker makes any advances on senior encumbrances to protect the security of your note. Depending on the terms and conditions of the servicing contract, you may be obligated to repay any such advances made by the broker. (Note: There must be a servicing agent on multi-lender transactions.) The broker may not guarantee or imply to guarantee, or advance any payments to you unless a securities permit is obtained from the Department of Corporations.

CHECK APPROPRIATE STATEMENTS

☐ THERE ARE NO SERVICING ARRANGEMENTS *(Does not apply to multi-lender transactions.)* ☐ BROKER IS THE SERVICING AGENT

☐ ANOTHER QUALIFIED PARTY WILL SERVICE THE LOAN ☐ COPY OF THE SERVICING CONTRACT IS ATTACHED

IF BROKER IS NOT SERVICING AGENT, WHAT IS THE RELATIONSHIP BETWEEN THE BROKER AND SERVICER?

COST TO LENDER FOR SERVICING ARRANGEMENTS *(EXPRESS AS DOLLAR AMOUNT OR PERCENTAGE)*

PER ☐ MONTH ☐ YEAR ☐   PAYABLE ☐ MONTHLY ☐ ANNUALLY

NAME OF AUTHORIZED SERVICER, IF ANY

BUSINESS ADDRESS   TELEPHONE NUMBER

PART 6 — BORROWER INFORMATION

SOURCE OF INFORMATION

☐ BORROWER ☐ BROKER INQUIRY ☐ CREDIT REPORT ☐ OTHER (DESCRIBE)

NAME	CO-BORROWER'S NAME
RESIDENCE ADDRESS	CO-BORROWER'S RESIDENCE ADDRESS
OCCUPATION OR PROFESSION	CO-BORROWER'S OCCUPATION OR PROFESSION
CURRENT EMPLOYER	CO-BORROWER'S CURRENT EMPLOYER
HOW LONG EMPLOYED? AGE	HOW LONG EMPLOYED? CO-BORROWER'S AGE

SOURCES OF GROSS INCOME (LIST AND IDENTIFY EACH SOURCE SEPARATELY.)	MONTHLY AMOUNT	CO-BORROWER SOURCES OF GROSS INCOME (LIST AND IDENTIFY EACH SOURCE SEPARATELY.)	MONTHLY AMOUNT
Gross Salary	$	Gross Salary	$
OTHER INCOME INCLUDING: Interest	$	OTHER INCOME INCLUDING: Interest	$
Dividends	$	Dividends	$
Gross Rental Income	$	Gross Rental Income	$
Miscellaneous Income	$	Miscellaneous Income	$

TOTAL EXPENSES OF ALL BORROWERS *(DO NOT COMPLETE IF BORROWER IS A CORPORATION)*

Payment of Loan being obtained	$	Spousal/Child Support	$
Rent	$	Insurance	$
Charge Account/Credit Cards	$	Vehicle Loan(s)	$
Mortgage Payments (include taxes and property insurance)	$	Other *(federal & state income taxes, etc.)*	$
TOTAL GROSS MONTHLY INCOME OF BORROWER(S) $		TOTAL MONTHLY EXPENSES OF BORROWER(S) $	

The borrower has filed for bankruptcy in the past 12 months. .... ☐ Yes ☐ No

If YES, the bankruptcy has been discharged or dismissed. .... ☐ Yes ☐ No

❖ **THE FOLLOWING STATEMENTS ONLY APPLY IF THE BORROWER IS A CORPORATION, PARTNERSHIP OR SOME OTHER FORM OF OPERATING BUSINESS ENTITY.**

Copies of a balance sheet of the entity and income statement covering the indicated period have been supplied by the borrower/obligor and are attached. If no, explain on addendum. .... ☐ Yes ☐ No

If YES, Date of balance sheet .... _____

Income statement period *(from-to)* .... _____

Financial Statements have been audited by CPA or PA. .... ☐ Yes ☐ No

Additional information is included on an attached addendum .... ☐ Yes ☐ No

PART 7	PROPERTY INFORMATION

Identification of property which is security for note. *(If no street address, the assessor's parcel number or legal description and a means for locating the property is attached.)*

(CHECK IF APPLICABLE)
☐ THERE IS MORE THAN ONE PROPERTY SECURING THE LOAN. IF MULTI-LENDER LOAN, YOU SHOULD REFER TO ATTACHED RE 851D.

STREET ADDRESS   OWNER OCCUPIED ☐ NO ☐ YES

ANNUAL PROPERTY TAXES	ARE TAXES DELINQUENT?	IF YES, AMT. REQUIRED TO BRING CURRENT
$ ☐ ACTUAL ☐ ESTIMATED	☐ NO ☐ YES	$

SOURCE OF TAX INFORMATION

PART 8	APPRAISAL INFORMATION

Estimate of fair market value is to be determined by an independent appraisal, copy of which must be provided to you prior to you obligating funds to make the loan. Note: You may waive the requirement of an independent appraisal, in writing, on a case by case basis, in which case the broker must provide a written estimate of fair market value. The broker must provide you, the investor, with the objective data upon which the broker's estimate is based. **In the case of a construction or rehabilitation loan, an appraisal must be completed by an independent, qualified appraiser in accordance with the Uniform Standards of Professional Appraisal Practice (USPAP).**

(CHECK IF APPLICABLE)
☐ THERE IS MORE THAN ONE PROPERTY SECURING THE LOAN. IF MULTI-LENDER LOAN REFER TO ATTACHED RE 851D.

FAIR MARKET VALUE (ACCORDING TO APPRAISER) *(Place this figure or brokers estimate of fair market value on line "F" of Part 10.)*	DATE OF APPRAISAL
$	
NAME OF APPRAISER (IF KNOWN TO BROKER)	PAST AND/OR CURRENT RELATIONSHIP OF APPRAISER TO BROKER (EMPLOYEE, AGENT, INDEPENDENT CONTRACTOR, ETC.)

ADDRESS OF APPRAISER

DESCRIPTION OF PROPERTY/IMPROVEMENT	IS THERE ADDITIONAL SECURING PROPERTY? ☐ YES IF YES, SEE ADDENDUM. ☐ NO

AGE	SQUARE FEET	TYPE OF CONSTRUCTION

IF THE PROPERTY IS CURRENTLY GENERATING INCOME FOR THE BORROWER/OBLIGOR:

ESTIMATED GROSS ANNUAL INCOME	ESTIMATED NET ANNUAL INCOME
$	$

PART 9   **ENCUMBRANCE INFORMATION**

Information is being provided concerning senior encumbrances against the property, to the extent reasonably available from customary sources (excluding the note described on page 1 Part 3). **Note:** You have the option to purchase a policy of title insurance or an endorsement to an existing policy of title insurance to insure your interest. You are entitled to a copy of a written loan application and a credit report to obtain information concerning all encumbrances which constitute liens against the property. This information may help determine the financial standing and creditworthiness of the borrower.

(CHECK IF APPLICABLE)

☐ THERE IS MORE THAN ONE PROPERTY SECURING THE LOAN. IF MULTI-LENDER LOAN, YOU SHOULD REFER TO ATTACHED RE 851D.

SOURCE OF INFORMATION

☐ BROKER INQUIRY   ☐ BORROWER   ☐ OTHER *(EXPLAIN)*

Are there any encumbrances of record against the securing property at this time?............... ☐ YES   ☐ NO

A. Over the last 12 months were any payments more than 60 days late? .... ☐ YES   ☐ NO

B. If YES, how many? ....

C. Do any of these payments remain unpaid?.. ☐ YES   ☐ NO

D. If YES, will the proceeds of subject loan be used to cure the delinquency? .... ☐ YES   ☐ NO

E. If NO, source of funds to bring the loan current. ....

Encumbrances remaining and/or expected or anticipated to be placed against the property by the borrower/obligor after the close of escrow (excluding the note described on page 1).

ENCUMBRANCE(S) REMAINING *(AS REPRESENTED BY THE BORROWER)*

PRIORITY (1ST, 2ND, ETC.)	INTEREST RATE %	PRIORITY (1ST, 2ND, ETC.)	INTEREST RATE %
BENEFICIARY		BENEFICIARY	
ORIGINAL AMOUNT $	APPROXIMATE PRINCIPAL BALANCE $	ORIGINAL AMOUNT $	APPROXIMATE PRINCIPAL BALANCE $
MONTHLY PAYMENT $	MATURITY DATE	MONTHLY PAYMENT $	MATURITY DATE
BALLOON PAYMENT ☐ YES ☐ NO ☐ UNKNOWN	IF YES, AMOUNT $	BALLOON PAYMENT ☐ YES ☐ NO ☐ UNKNOWN	IF YES, AMOUNT $

ENCUMBRANCES EXPECTED OR ANTICIPATED *(AS REPRESENTED BY THE BORROWER)*

PRIORITY (1ST, 2ND, ETC.)	INTEREST RATE %	PRIORITY (1ST, 2ND, ETC.)	INTEREST RATE %
BENEFICIARY		BENEFICIARY	
ORIGINAL AMOUNT $	MATURITY DATE	ORIGINAL AMOUNT $	MATURITY DATE
MONTHLY PAYMENT $		MONTHLY PAYMENT $	
BALLOON PAYMENT ☐ YES ☐ NO ☐ UNKNOWN	IF YES, AMOUNT $	BALLOON PAYMENT ☐ YES ☐ NO ☐ UNKNOWN	IF YES, AMOUNT $

Additional remaining, expected or anticipated encumbrances are set forth in an attachment to this statement. .... ☐ Yes   ☐ No

PART 10   **LOAN TO VALUE RATIO**

(CHECK IF APPLICABLE)

☐ THERE IS MORE THAN ONE PROPERTY SECURING THE LOAN. IF MULTI-LENDER LOAN, YOU SHOULD REFER TO ATTACHED RE 851D.

A. Remaining encumbrances senior to this loan *(from part 8)* .... $ _____

B. Encumbrances expected or anticipated senior to this loan
    (from part 9) .... + $ _____

C. Total remaining and expected or anticipated encumbrances senior to this loan .... = $ _____

D. Principal amount of this loan from page 1 part 3 .... + $ _____

E. Total all senior encumbrances and this loan .... = $ _____

F. Fair market value from page 4 part 8 .... ÷ $ _____

G. Loan to value ratio .... = _____ %

Note: See Part 4 if multi-lender transaction.

BROKER VERIFICATION

The information in this statement and in the attachments hereto is true and correct to the best of my knowledge and belief.

SIGNATURE OF BROKER OR DESIGNATED REPRESENTATIVE	BROKER/CORPORATION ID#	DATE
➤		

ACKNOWLEDGMENT OF RECEIPT

The prospective lender/purchaser acknowledges receipt of a copy of this statement signed by or on behalf of the broker.

SIGNATURE OF PROSPECTIVE LENDER/PURCHASER	DATE
➤	

For licensing information, please refer to the Department of Real Estate's Web site located at www.dre.ca.gov.

or

You may call the DRE licensing information telephone number at (916) 227-0931.

STATE OF CALIFORNIA

DEPARTMENT OF REAL ESTATE
MORTGAGE LENDING

LENDER/PURCHASER DISCLOSURE STATEMENT
(Sale of Existing Note)

RE 851B (Rev. 2/04)

DISCLOSURE STATEMENT SUMMARY

Note: If this is a multi-lender transaction and more than one property secures the loan, you should also refer to attached Lender/Purchaser Disclosure Statement Multi-Property (Cross Collateralization) Addendum (RE 851D).

BALANCE OF NOTE YOU ARE RECEIVING *(SEE PART 3)*	MARKET VALUE OF PROPERTY (SEE PART 8)	TOTAL AMOUNT OF ENCUMBRANCES SENIOR TO THIS LOAN *(SEE PART 9)*
$	$	$
PROTECTIVE EQUITY (MARKET VALUE MINUS THIS LOAN AND TOTAL SENIOR ENCUMBRANCES)	TOTAL LOAN TO VALUE (SEE PART 10E)	
$	%	

PART 1 — BROKER INFORMATION

NAME OF BROKER	REAL ESTATE LICENSE ID#
BUSINESS ADDRESS	TELEPHONE NUMBER

NAME OF BROKERS REPRESENTATIVE

PART 2 — BROKER CAPACITY IN TRANSACTION

THE BROKER IDENTIFIED IN PART 1 OF THIS STATEMENT IS ACTING IN THE FOLLOWING CAPACITY IN THIS TRANSACTION: (CHECK AS APPLIES)

☐ A. Agent in arranging a sale of an existing note on behalf of another.
☐ B. Principal as owner and seller of an existing note.
☐ C. Agent and/or principal arranging the sale of a portion of an existing note. *(Multi-lender transactions are subject to Business and Professions Code Section 10238.)*

PART 3 — TRANSACTION INFORMATION

(CHECK IF APPLICABLE)

☐ THERE IS MORE THAN ONE PROPERTY SECURING THE LOAN. IF MULTI-LENDER LOAN, YOU SHOULD ALSO REFER TO ATTACHED RE 851D.

SOURCE OF INFORMATION ABOUT THIS EXISTING NOTE:

☐ BROKER INQUIRY   ☐ BORROWER   ☐ SELLER OF NOTE   ☐ OTHER (DESCRIBE)

NAME OF EXISTING NOTE OWNER

ORIGINAL PRINCIPAL	SELLING PRICE	YOUR SHARE IF MULTI-LENDER TRANS.	DATE OF NOTE
$	$	$	
PRIORITY OF THIS NOTE (1st, 2nd)	MATURITY DATE	DATE INTEREST PAID TO	/////////
INTEREST RATE ___% ☐ VARIABLE ☐ FIXED	PERCENT OF PREMIUM OVER OR DISCOUNT FROM THE PRINCIPAL BALANCE PLUS ACCRUED BUT UNPAID INTEREST. ___%		EFF. RATE OF RETURN ___% [If note is paid according to its term (multi-lender transactions only).]
PAYMENT DUE DATE	AMOUNT OF PAYMENT $	YOUR SHARE OF PYMT. IF MULTI-LENDER TRANSACTION $	PAYMENT FREQUENCY ☐ MONTHLY ☐ WEEKLY
BALLOON PAYMENT ☐ YES ☐ NO	AMOUNT OF BALLOON PAYMENT $	YOUR SHARE OF BALLOON PAYMENT IF MULTI-LENDER TRANSACTION $	*AN ASSIGNMENT OF THE TRUST DEED WILL BE RECORDED*
UNPAID PRINCIPAL BALANCE $	YOUR SHARE OF UNPAID PRINCIPAL BALANCE IF MULTI-LENDER TRANSACTION $	(CHECK ONE) ☐ AMORTIZED ☐ PARTIALLY AMORTIZED	☐ INTEREST ONLY

Balloon Payment

A balloon payment is any installment payment (usually the payment due at maturity) which is greater than twice the amount of the smallest installment payment under the terms of the promissory note or sales contract.

The borrower/vendee may have to obtain a new loan or sell the property to make the balloon payment. If the effort is not successful it may be necessary for the holder of the note/contract to foreclose on the property as a means of collecting the amount owed.

Over the last 12 months were any payments more than 60 days late? .... ☐ Yes ☐ No
    If YES, how many? ....

Have the delinquencies been cured? .... ☐ Yes ☐ No
    If NO, what is the amount required to bring current? .... $ _____

There are subordination provisions. .... ☐ Yes ☐ No
    If YES, explain here or on an attachment.

PART 4	MULTI-LENDER TRANSACTIONS

NAME OF ESCROW HOLDER	ANTICIPATED CLOSING DATE

ADDRESS OF ESCROW HOLDER

ESTIMATED LENDER COSTS

	$ _____
	$ _____
	$ _____
TOTAL	$ _____

Servicing
You will be a joint beneficiary with others on this note and you should request a list of names and addresses of the beneficiaries as of the close of escrow from the broker or servicing agent. The beneficiary(ies) holding more than 50% interest in the note may govern the actions to be taken on behalf of all holders in the event of default or other matters. See Civil Code Section 2941.9.

Loan To Value
GENERALLY the aggregate principal amount of the notes or interests sold, together with the unpaid principal amount of any encumbrances upon the real property senior thereto, shall not exceed the following percentages of the current market value of the real property as determined in writing by the broker or qualified appraiser.

Single–family residence, owner–occupied 80%
Single–family residence, not owner–occupied 75%
Commercial and income–producing properties 65%
Single-family residentially zoned lot or parcel which has installed off-site improvements including
    drainage, curbs, gutters, sidewalks, paved roads, and utilities as mandated by the political
    subdivision having jurisdiction over the lot or parcel 65%
Land which has been zoned for (and if required, approved for subdivision as) commercial or
    residential development 50%
Other real property 35%

The percentage amounts specified above may be exceeded when and to the extent that the broker determines that the encumbrance of the property in excess of these percentages is reasonable and prudent considering all relevant factors pertaining to the real property. However, in no event shall the aggregate principal amount of the notes or interests sold, together with the unpaid principal amount of any encumbrances upon the property senior thereto, exceed 80 percent of the current fair market value of improved real property or 50 percent of the current fair market value of unimproved real property, except in the case of a single-family residentially zoned lot or parcel as defined above, which shall not exceed 65% of current fair market value of that lot or parcel. A written statement shall be prepared by the broker that sets forth the material considerations and facts that the broker relies upon for his or her determination which shall be disclosed to the lender or note purchaser(s) and retained as a part of the broker's record of the transaction.

NOTE: If more than one property secures this loan, you should also refer to attached RE 851D.

PART 5 — SERVICING ARRANGEMENTS

If the loan is to be serviced by a real estate broker you must be notified within ten (10) days if the broker makes any advances on senior encumbrances to protect the security of your note. Depending on the terms and conditions of the servicing contract, you may be obligated to repay any such advances made by the broker. The broker may not guarantee or imply to guarantee, or advance any payments to you unless a securities permit is obtained from the Department of Corporations.

CHECK APPROPRIATE STATEMENTS

☐ THERE ARE NO SERVICING ARRANGEMENTS *(Does not apply to multi-lender transactions.)*
☐ ANOTHER QUALIFIED PARTY WILL SERVICE THE LOAN

☐ BROKER IS THE SERVICING AGENT
☐ COPY OF THE SERVICING CONTRACT IS ATTACHED

IF BROKER IS NOT SERVICING AGENT, WHAT IS THE RELATIONSHIP BETWEEN THE BROKER AND SERVICER?

COST TO LENDER FOR SERVICING ARRANGEMENTS *(EXPRESS AS DOLLAR AMOUNT OR PERCENTAGE)*

PER ☐ MONTH ☐ YEAR   PAYABLE ☐ MONTHLY ☐ ANNUALLY

NAME OF AUTHORIZED SERVICER, IF ANY

BUSINESS ADDRESS

TELEPHONE NUMBER

PART 6 — TRUSTOR/OBLIGOR INFORMATION *(as known to broker)*

If the broker made, arranged, or serviced the loan or if any of the information is known to the broker or is available from the seller of the note, complete this part.

SOURCE OF INFORMATION

☐ TRUSTOR   ☐ SELLER OF NOTE   ☐ BROKER (BROKER MADE, ARRANGED OR SERVICED THE LOAN)
☐ CREDIT REPORT   ☐ OTHER (DESCRIBE)

NAME	CO-TRUSTOR'S NAME
RESIDENCE ADDRESS	CO-TRUSTOR'S RESIDENCE ADDRESS
OCCUPATION OR PROFESSION	CO-TRUSTOR'S OCCUPATION OR PROFESSION
CURRENT EMPLOYER	CO-TRUSTOR'S CURRENT EMPLOYER
HOW LONG EMPLOYED? AGE	HOW LONG EMPLOYED? CO-TRUSTOR'S AGE

SOURCES OF GROSS INCOME *(LIST AND IDENTIFY EACH SOURCE SEPARATELY.)*	MONTHLY AMOUNT	CO-TRUSTOR SOURCES OF GROSS INCOME *(LIST AND IDENTIFY EACH SOURCE SEPARATELY.)*	MONTHLY AMOUNT
Gross salary	$	Gross salary	$
OTHER INCOME INCLUDING: Interest	$	OTHER INCOME INCLUDING: Interest	$
Dividends	$	Dividends	$
Gross rental income	$	Gross rental income	$
Miscellaneous income	$	Miscellaneous income	$

TOTAL EXPENSES OF ALL TRUSTORS *(DO NOT COMPLETE IF TRUSTOR IS A CORPORATION)*

Payment of loan being obtained	$	Spousal/child support	$
Rent	$	Insurance	$
Charge account/credit cards	$	Vehicle loan(s)	$
Mortgage payments *(include taxes and property insurance)*	$	Other *(federal & state income taxes, etc.)*	$
TOTAL GROSS MONTHLY INCOME OF TRUSTOR(S) $		TOTAL MONTHLY EXPENSES OF TRUSTOR(S) $	

The trustor has filed for bankruptcy in the past 12 months. .... ☐ Yes ☐ No
☐ Unknown

If YES, the bankruptcy has been discharged or dismissed. .... ☐ Yes ☐ No
☐ Unknown

❖ **THE FOLLOWING STATEMENTS ONLY APPLY IF THE TRUSTOR IS A CORPORATION, PARTNERSHIP OR SOME OTHER FORM OF OPERATING BUSINESS ENTITY.**

Copies of a balance sheet of the entity and income statement covering the indicated period have been supplied by the trustor/obligor and are attached. If no, explain on addendum. .... ☐ Yes ☐ No

If YES, date of balance sheet. .... _____

Income statement period *(from-to)* .... _____

Financial statements have been audited by CPA or PA. .... ☐ Yes ☐ No

Additional information is included on an attached addendum .... ☐ Yes ☐ No

_____
_____
_____
_____
_____

PART 7   **PROPERTY INFORMATION** *(if known to broker)*

Identification of property which is security for note. *(If no street address, the assessor's parcel number or legal description and a means for locating the property is attached.)*

(CHECK IF APPLICABLE)
☐ THERE IS MORE THAN ONE PROPERTY SECURING THE LOAN. IF MULTI-LENDER LOAN, YOU SHOULD ALSO REFER TO ATTACHED RE 851D.

STREET ADDRESS	OWNER OCCUPIED
	☐ NO ☐ YES

ANNUAL PROPERTY TAXES			ARE TAXES DELINQUENT?	IF YES, AMT. REQUIRED TO BRING CURRENT
$	☐ ACTUAL	☐ ESTIMATED	☐ NO ☐ YES	$

SOURCE OF TAX INFORMATION

| **PART 8** | **APPRAISAL INFORMATION** |

Estimate of fair market value is to be determined by an independent appraisal, a copy of which must be provided to you prior to you obligating funds to make the loan. Note: You may waive the requirement of an independent appraisal, in writing, on a case by case basis, in which case the broker must provide a written estimate of fair market value. The broker must provide you, the investor, with the objective data upon which the broker's estimate is based. **In the case of a construction or rehabilitation loan, an appraisal must be completed by an independent, qualified appraiser in accordance with the Uniform Standards of Professional Appraisal Practice (USPAP).**

(CHECK IF APPLICABLE)
☐ THERE IS MORE THAN ONE PROPERTY SECURING THE LOAN. IF MULTI-LENDER LOAN, YOU SHOULD ALSO REFER TO ATTACHED RE 851D.

FAIR MARKET VALUE (ACCORDING TO APPRAISER)
$

DATE OF APPRAISAL

NAME OF APPRAISER (IF KNOWN TO BROKER)

PAST AND/OR CURRENT RELATIONSHIP OF APPRAISER TO BROKER
(EMPLOYEE, AGENT, INDEPENDENT CONTRACTOR, ETC.)

ADDRESS OF APPRAISER

DESCRIPTION OF PROPERTY/IMPROVEMENT

IS THERE ADDITIONAL SECURING PROPERTY?
☐ YES   IF YES, SEE ADDENDUM.
☐ NO

| AGE | SQUARE FEET | TYPE OF CONSTRUCTION |

IF THE PROPERTY IS CURRENTLY GENERATING INCOME FOR THE BORROWER/OBLIGOR:

ESTIMATED GROSS ANNUAL INCOME
$

ESTIMATED NET ANNUAL INCOME
$

OTHER INFORMATION KNOWN TO BROKER

| **PART 9** | **ENCUMBRANCE INFORMATION** |

Information is being provided concerning senior encumbrances against the property, to the extent reasonably available from customary sources (excluding the note described on page 1 Part 3). **Note:** You have the option to purchase a policy of title insurance or an endorsement to an existing policy of title insurance to insure your interest. You are entitled to a copy of a written loan application and a credit report to obtain information concerning all encumbrances which constitute liens against the property. This information may help determine the financial standing and creditworthiness of the borrower.

(CHECK IF APPLICABLE)
☐ THERE IS MORE THAN ONE PROPERTY SECURING THE LOAN. IF MULTI-LENDER LOAN, YOU SHOULD ALSO REFER TO ATTACHED RE 851D.

SOURCE OF INFORMATION
☐ TRUSTOR   ☐ BROKER INQUIRY   ☐ EXISTING BENEFICIARY   OTHER (EXPLAIN)

SENIOR ENCUMBRANCE(S) REMAINING

PRIORITY (1ST, 2ND, ETC.)	INTEREST RATE %	PRIORITY (1ST, 2ND, ETC.)	INTEREST RATE %
BENEFICIARY		BENEFICIARY	
ORIGINAL AMOUNT $	APPROXIMATE PRINCIPAL BALANCE $	ORIGINAL AMOUNT $	APPROXIMATE PRINCIPAL BALANCE $
MONTHLY PAYMENT $	MATURITY DATE	MONTHLY PAYMENT $	MATURITY DATE
BALLOON PAYMENT ☐ YES ☐ NO ☐ UNKNOWN	IF YES, AMOUNT $	BALLOON PAYMENT ☐ YES ☐ NO ☐ UNKNOWN	IF YES, AMOUNT $

Are there additional remaining senior encumbrances? .... ☐ YES   ☐ NO
   If YES, they are set forth in an attachment to this statement.
Has the seller received notice of default on any senior encumbrances in the last 12 months? . ☐ YES   ☐ NO
   If YES, has default been cured? .... ☐ YES   ☐ NO
Is the broker aware of any junior encumbrances? .... ☐ YES   ☐ NO
   If YES, they are set forth in an attachment to this statement. .... ☐ YES   ☐ NO

FINANCIAL
TITLE COMPANY

PRELIMINARY REPORT

Mortgage Broker

Branch:
4982 Cherry Ave
San Jose, CA 95118
Phone: (408) 445-3700   Fax: (408) 445-3710
Contact: **Jodi Holloway.**
Escrow Contact:

Property Address:

1234 Nice House Way
San Jose, CA 95120

Order Number: 91574-J
Other Reference:
Buyer/Borrower:
Robert Borrower and Mary Borrower:

1. In response to the above referenced application for a policy of title insurance, this Company reports that it is prepared to issue, or cause to be issued, as of the date hereof, a Policy or Policies of Title Insurance describing the land and the estate or interest therein hereinafter set forth, insuring against loss which may be sustained by reason of any defect, lien or encumbrance not shown or referred to as an Exception herein or not excluded from coverage pursuant to the printed Schedules, Conditions and Stipulations of said Policy forms. The printed Exceptions and Exclusions from the coverage of said Policy or Policies are set forth in Exhibit A attached.

Please read the exceptions shown or referred to below and the Exceptions and Exclusions set forth in Exhibit A of this report carefully. The exceptions and exclusions are meant to provide you with notice of matters which are not covered under the terms of the title insurance policy and should be carefully considered.

It is important to note that this preliminary report is not a written representation as to the condition of title and may not list all liens, defects, and encumbrances affecting title to the land. This report (and any supplements hereto) is issued solely for the purpose of facilitating the issuance of a policy of title insurance and no liability is assumed hereby. If it is desired that liability be assumed prior to the issuance of a policy of title insurance, a Binder or Commitment should be requested.

The form of policy of title insurance contemplated by this report is:

2. **ALTA Lender's Policy**

Dated as of **February 21, 2007** at 7:30 a.m.

3. The estate or interest in the land hereinafter described or referred to covered by this Report is:

A Fee

4. Title to said estate or interest at the date hereof is vested in:

Robert Borrower and Mary Borrower, Husband and wife as Joint Tenants

Page No. 2
Order No.

LEGAL DESCRIPTION

5. The land referred to in this Report is described as follows:

All that certain real property situated in the City of San Jose, County of Santa Clara, State of California, described as follows:

Lot 38, as shown on the Map entitled,   **"Saint Patrick Park**   , which Map was filed for record on July 23, 1959 in Book 109, Page(s) 39 of Maps, Records of Santa Clara County.

EXCEPTING THEREFROM the underground water or rights thereto, with no right of surface entry, as granted to San Jose Water Works, a California Corporation by Instrument recorded August 28, 1959 in Book 4528, Page 434, Official Records.

APN: 115-143-001

Page No. 3
Order No.

6. **At the date hereof exceptions to coverage in addition to the printed Exceptions and Exclusions in said policy would be as follows:**

EXCEPTIONS:

7. 1. General and special taxes and assessments for the fiscal year 2007-2008, a lien not yet due or payable.

8. 2. General and special taxes and assessments for the fiscal year 2006-2007.

First Installment:	$2,309.86 Paid
Second Installment:	$2,309.86 Open
Tax Rate Area:	17-076
A. P. No.:	115-143-001

8. 3. The lien of supplemental taxes, if any, assessed pursuant to Chapter 3.5 commencing with Section 75 of the California Revenue and Taxation Code.

9. 4. An easement shown or dedicated on the Map as referred to in the legal description

For:	Public service and incidental purposes.
Affects:	The Westerly 5 feet of the premises

For:	Wire Clearance and incidental purposes.
Affects:	The Easterly 5 feet of the Westerly 10 feet of the premises

9. 5. Building setback line 20 feet from Harlow Way as shown on the filed map.

10. 6. Covenants, conditions, restrictions and easements in the document recorded **July 27, 1959, in Book 4494, Page 45** of Official Records, which provide that a violation thereof shall not defeat or render invalid the lien of any first mortgage or deed of trust made in good faith and for value, but deleting any covenant, condition or restriction indicating a preference, limitation or discrimination based on race, color, religion, sex, handicap, familial status, national origin, sexual orientation, marital status, ancestry, source of income or disability, to the extent such covenants, conditions or restrictions violate Title 42, Section 3604(c), of the United States Codes or Section 12955 of the California Government Code. Lawful restrictions under state and federal law on the age of occupants in senior housing or housing for older persons shall not be construed as restrictions based on familial status

11. 7. Deed of Trust securing payment of the amount hereinafter set forth and any other amounts payable under the terms thereof

Dated:	October 24, 2004
Amount:	$100,000.00
Trustor:	Robert Borrower and Mary Borrower, Husband and wife
Trustee:	Handy Trustee Company, a California Corporation
Beneficiary:	New Lender Corporation, A California Corporation
Loan Number:	98856785
Recorded:	November 13, 2004, in Book 20041113, Page 2349, Official Records

Page No.
Order No.

NOTES:

12.   ***Privacy Promise For Customers***

We will not reveal non-public personal customer information to any
external non-affiliated organization unless we have been authorized
by the customer, or are required by law.

Occasionally, due to certain market conditions, it may not be possible to deliver policies of title insurance in a
time frame that our clients request. Should you have individual needs please contact the title operation that
issued this report. We recognize, appreciate and understand your needs.

a.   STR applies: YES

b.   This report does not reflect requests for notice of default, requests for notice of delinquency, subsequent
transfers of easements, and similar matters not germane to the issuance of the policy of title insurance
anticipated hereunder.

c.   If this company is requested to disburse funds in connection with this transaction, Chapter 598 of 1989
Mandates of the California Insurance Code requires hold periods for checks deposited to escrow or sub-
escrow accounts. Such periods vary depending upon the type of check and anticipated methods of
deposit should be discussed with the escrow officer.

d.   No endorsement issued in connection with the policy and relating to covenants, conditions or restrictions
provides coverage for environmental protection.

e.   Our investigation has been completed and the improvements located on the land described herein is a
single family residence known as 1234 **Nice House Way, San Jose, CA 95120**

At the close of escrow, an ALTA Lenders Policy of Title Insurance will be issued with 100 and 116
series Endorsements.

f.   If the land is an improved residential lot on which there is located a one-to-four family residence and
each insured buyer is a natural person, and unless otherwise directed, we will issue the extended
coverage CLTA Homeowners Policy of Title Insurance (6/2/98).

g.   According to the public records, there has been no conveyance of the land within a period of twenty-four
months prior to the date of this report, except as follows:

A document recorded October 30, 2006 as Series No.   **20040711** Official Records.

From: **Elizabeth Predecessor and Ted Predecessor, wife and husband**
To: **Robert Borrower and Mary Borrower, Husband and wife**

**This order was generated by Financial Title Company. All questions and recordings should be
directed to:**

**3130 Crow Canyon Place, Suite 300
San Ramon, CA 94583
Phone No.:   (925) 242-5600
Fax No.:   (925) 328-1546**

EXHIBIT "A"

13.

LIST OF PRINTED EXCEPTIONS AND EXCLUSIONS

CLTA Preliminary Report Form
(Rev. 6/98)

CLTA PRELIMINARY REPORT FORM
LIST OF PRINTED EXCEPTIONS AND EXCLUSIONS

SCHEDULE B

1. CALIFORNIA LAND TITLE ASSOCIATION STANDARD COVERAGE POLICY FORM - 1990
AND
CALIFORNIA LAND TITLE ASSOCIATION HOMEOWNER'S POLICY - EAGLE (6/2/98)
EXCLUSIONS FROM COVERAGE

In addition to the Exceptions in Schedule B, you are not insured against loss, costs, attorneys' fees, and expenses resulting from:

1. Governmental police power, and the existence of violation of any law or government regulation. This includes ordinances, laws and regulations concerning:
   a. building
   b. zoning
   c. land use
   d. improvements on the land
   e. land division
   f. environmental protection
   This Exclusion does not apply to violations or the enforcement of these matters if notice of the violation or enforcement appears in the Public Records at the Policy Date.
   This Exclusion does not limit the coverage described in Covered Risk 14, 15, 16, 17 or 24.
2. The failure of your existing structures, or any part of them, to be constructed in accordance with applicable building codes. This Exclusion does not apply to violations of building codes if notice of the violation appears in the Public Records at the Policy Date.
3. The right to take the land by condemning it, unless:
   a. a notice of exercising the right appears in the Public Records at the Policy Date; or
   b. the taking happened before the Policy Date and is binding on you if you bought the land without knowing of the taking.
4. Risks:
   a. that are created, allowed or agreed to by you, whether or not they appear in the Public Records;
   b. that are known to you at the Policy Date, but not to us, unless they appear in the Public Records at the Policy Date;
   c. that result in no loss to you; or
   d. that first occur after the Policy Date - this does not limit the coverage described in Covered Risk 7, 8.d, 22, 23, 24, or 25.
5. Failure to pay value for your title.
6. Lack of a right:
   a. to any land outside the area specifically described and referred to in paragraph 3 of Schedule A; and
   b. in streets, alleys, or waterways that touch the land.
   This Exclusion does not limit the coverage described in Covered Risk 11 or 18.

2. AMERICAN LAND TITLE ASSOCIATION LOAN POLICY (10-17-92)
WITH ALTA ENDORSEMENT - FORM 1 COVERAGE

The following matters are expressly excluded from the coverage of this policy and the Company will not pay loss or damage, costs, attorneys' fees or expenses which arise by reason of:

1. (a) Any law, ordinance or governmental regulation (including but not limited to building and zoning laws, ordinances, or regulations) restricting, regulating, prohibiting or relating to (i) the occupancy, use, or enjoyment of the land; (ii) the character, dimensions or location of any improvement now or hereafter erected on the land; (iii) a separation in ownership or a change in the dimensions or area of the land or any parcel of which the land is or was a part; or (iv) environmental protection, or the effect of any violation of these laws, ordinances or governmental regulations, except to the extent that a notice of the enforcement thereof or a notice of a defect, lien or encumbrance resulting from a violation or alleged violation affecting the land has been recorded in the public records at Date of Policy.

Any governmental police power not excluded by (a) above, except to the extent that a notice of the exercise thereof or a notice of a defect, lien or encumbrance resulting from a violation or alleged violation affecting the land has been recorded in the public records at Date of Policy.

EXHIBIT "A" - CONTINUED

2. Rights of eminent domain unless notice of the exercise thereof has been recorded in the public records at Date of Policy, but not excluding from coverage any taking which has occurred prior to Date of Policy which would be binding on the rights of a purchaser for value without knowledge.

3. Defects, liens, encumbrances, adverse claims or other matters:

    (a) created, suffered, assumed or agreed to by the insured claimant;

    (b) not known to the Company, not recorded in the public records at Date of Policy, but known to the insured claimant and not disclosed in writing to the Company by the insured claimant prior to the date the insured claimant became an insured under this policy;

    (c) resulting in no loss or damage to the insured claimant;

    (d) attaching or created subsequent to Date of Policy (except to the extent that this policy insures the priority of the lien of the insured mortgage

    over any statutory lien for services, labor or material or to the extent insurance is afforded herein as to assessments for street improvements under construction or completed at Date of Policy); or

    (e) resulting in loss or damage which would not have been sustained if the insured claimant had paid value for the insured mortgage.

4. Unenforceability of the lien of the insured mortgage because of the inability or failure of the insured at Date of Policy, or the inability or failure of any subsequent owner of the indebtedness, to comply with applicable doing business laws of the state in which the land is situated.

5. Invalidity or unenforceability of the lien of the insured mortgage, or claim thereof, which arises out of the transaction evidenced by the insured mortgage and is based upon usury or any consumer credit protection or truth in lending law.

6. Any statutory lien for services, labor or materials (or the claim of priority of any statutory lien for services, labor or materials over the lien of the insured mortgage) arising from an improvement or work related to the land which is contracted for and commenced subsequent to Date of Policy and is not financed in whole or in part by proceeds of the indebtedness secured by the insured mortgage which at Date of Policy the insured has advanced or is obligated to advance.

7. Any claim, which arises out of the transaction creating the interest of the mortgagee insured by this policy, by reason of the operation of federal bankruptcy, state insolvency, or similar creditors' rights laws, that is based on:

    (a) the transaction creating the interest of the insured mortgagee being deemed a fraudulent conveyance or fraudulent transfer; or

    (b) the subordination of the interest of the insured mortgagee as a result of the application of the doctrine of equitable subordination; or

    (c) the transaction creating the interest of the insured mortgagee being deemed a preferential transfer except where the preferential transfer results from the failure: (i) to timely record the instrument of transfer; or (ii) of such recordation to impart notice to a purchaser for value or a judgment or lien creditor.

The above policy forms may be issued to afford either Standard Coverage or Extended Coverage. In addition to the above Exclusions from Coverage, the Exceptions from Coverage in a Standard Coverage policy will also include the following General Exceptions:

EXCEPTIONS FROM COVERAGE

This policy does not insure against loss or damage (and the Company will not pay costs, attorneys' fees or expenses) which arise by reason of:

1. Taxes or assessments which are not shown as existing liens by the records of any taxing authority that levies taxes or assessments on real property or by the public records.

2. Proceedings by a public agency which may result in taxes or assessments, or notices of such proceedings, whether or not shown by the records of such agency or by the public records.

3. Any facts, rights, interests or claims which are not shown by the public records but which could be ascertained by an inspection of the land or by making inquiry of persons in possession thereof.

4. Easements, liens or encumbrances, or claims thereof, which are not shown by the public records.

5. Discrepancies, conflicts in boundary lines, shortage in area, encroachments, or any other facts which a correct survey would disclose, and which are not shown by the public records.

6. (a) Unpatented mining claims; (b) reservations or exceptions in patents or in Acts authorizing the issuance thereof; (c) water rights, claims or title to water, whether or not the matters excepted under (a), (b), (c) are shown by the public records.

144

HOW TO READ A PRELIMINARY TITLE REPORT
EXPLANATION PAGE

1. This paragraph specifies that no liability is ever intended under a Preliminary Title Report, and further indicates what should be requested if the customer desires assumption of liability prior to policy issuance.

2. This date represents the date and time to which the public records have been examined.

3. This item indicates estate or interest covered by the Preliminary Report. A "fee" is the highest type of estate or interest an owner can haven in land, freely transferable and inheritable and whose owner is entitled to possession.

4. This the name(s) of the vested owner(s) as it appears in the public records, together with marital status and manner of holding title: Joint Tenants, Community Property, Tenants in Common, etc. or Corporate Status in the case of a corporation.

5. A legal description is a method of geographically identifying a parcel of land, which is acceptable in a court of law. All documents prepared in the transaction should contain the exact legal description as shown on the Preliminary Report.

6. Describes matters, which will exceptions to the policy coverage unless paid, released or otherwise eliminated.

7. Since taxes are a paramount lien, they will always be shown as the first exception in the Preliminary Report.

8. NOTE: The lien of county of city taxes on real property is superior to contract liens, thus the county or city real property tax lien is superior to the deed of trust.
   Effective July 1, 1983, the Supplemental Real Property Tax Assessment came into effect, therefore, all preliminary reports or title policies after that date must reflect this information.
   Supplemental tax bills originate when one of the following occurs:
   - Change of Ownership
   - Recent construction and/or improvements

9. Easements: In the orderly development of land, easements for many purposes are necessary to provide the services and facilities we all need, therefore, most parcels of land are burdened to some degree by easements passing through them; in subdivided lands these easements usually follow the lot lines and create no difficulties. An easement can be granted by way of deed or through a dedication on the Parcel/Tract Map.

10. Covenants, Conditions and Restrictions: In the orderly development of land, restrictions to the use of the land are necessary in order to maintain uniform standards of development. These types of covenants, conditions and restrictions will normally present no problem to a lender.

11. Deeds of Trust—all information pertaining to a specific loan including but not limited to the names of the trustor(s), date and amount of loan, Trustee and Beneficiary, loan number and date, book and page number of recorded documents.

12. Exhibit A – List of exceptions and exclusions. Standard to all Preliminary Reports.

13. Notes: Privacy Promise For Customers – A summary standard to all Preliminary Reports.

14. A map is provided to verify property location. No representations or warranties are made with respect ot he accuracy or completeness of the map. **(map NOT INCLUDED)**

THINGS TO LOOK FOR ON YOUR PRELIMINARY TITLE REPORT

TYPE OF ESTATE OR INTEREST (No. 3 on Sample)
- Fee Title or other (leasehold or equitable)

VESTED OWNERS NAME (No. 4 on Sample)
- Are the names the same as shown on the purchase agreement, deposit receipt and application?
- Have all parties executed and approved the purchase agreement?

LEGAL DESCRIPTION (No. 5 on Sample)
- A method of geographically identifying a parcel of land, by lot and block or metes and bounds.
- Also discloses assessors parcel number and joint plant number.

PRINTED EXCEPTIONS (No.'s 7 & 8 on Sample)
- Current taxes, supplemental taxes due to recent re-assessment, lien for future supplemental taxes, sale to state for unpaid delinquent taxes and/or bonds.

EASEMENTS (No. 9 on Sample)
- Understand the type and location of all easements
- Don't hesitate to ask your escrow officer or title officer for a copy of the recorded easements.

COVENANTES, CONDITIONS AND RESTRICTIONS (No. 10 on Sample)
- Declaration by owners of any subdivision prior to sale describing property restrictions and agreements said property and future owners.
- Copies of all recorded CC&R's are available upon request.

DEEDS OF TRUST (No. 11 on Sample)
- All existing loans against the property or the existence of any paid off loans, which have not yet been reconveyed of record.

NOTICE OF DEFAULT
- Alerts all parties f an existing foreclosure proceeding

STATE OR FEDERAL TAX LIENS, JUDGEMENTS AND BANKRUPTCY
- Any court proceedings affecting the seller and/or the property therein.

FIVE YEAR SHORT TERM RATE & REFINANCE RATE
- If applicable, a 20% savings is passed along to the buyer on properties insured by ANY title company within the past five years
- The refinance rate is a 30% discount to borrowers

PLAT MAP
- Describes a lot size, location of easements and identifies street name and nearest location.

NOTE SECURED BY A DEED OF TRUST

Loan Number: 20070307   Date: **Wednesday, March 07, 2007**   **Los Gatos, California**

123 ANY STREET
FREMONT CA 94539
Property Address

1. BORROWER'S PROMISE TO PAY

In return for a loan that I have received, I promise to pay U.S. **$170,000.00** (this amount will be called "principal"), plus interest, to the order of **SARATOGA BANCORP**, (who will be called "Lender"). I understand that the Lender may transfer this Note. The Lender or anyone else who takes this Note by transfer and who is entitled to receive payments under this Note will be called the "Note Holder(s)."

2. INTEREST

I will pay interest at a yearly rate as described in paragraph 3 below.

Interest commences on **Monday, March 12, 2007**, and, if paragraph 3 reflects more than one interest rate during the loan term, the rate will change on the date which is one (1) calendar month before each Payment Start Date.

Interest will be charged on unpaid principal until the full amount of principal has been paid.

I also agree to pay interest at the rate described in paragraph 3 below on the prepaid finance charges which are a part of the principal.

3. PAYMENTS

My payments are   [X] Interest Only   [ ] Fully Amortized   [ ] Other
I will make my payments each month as follows:

Number of Payments	Payment Start Dates	Interest Rates	Payment Amounts
60	Starting May 1, 2007	11.000%	$1,558.33
1	Starting May 1, 2012	11.000%	$171,558.33

I will make these payments until I have paid all of the principal and interest and any other charges that I may owe under this Note. If on **Tuesday, May 01, 2012** (the Due Date) I still owe amounts under this Note (balloon balance), I will pay all those amounts, in full, on that date.

I will make my payments payable to **J.A. FINANCIAL   301 LOS GATOS SARATOGA ROAD, SUITE 'A' LOS GATOS, CA 95130**, or at a different place if I am notified by the Note Holder or the Agent for the Note Holder.

4. BORROWER'S FAILURE TO PAY AS REQUIRED

(A) Late Charge For Overdue Payments. If I do not pay the full amount of each monthly payment by the end of ten calendar days after the date it is due, I will pay a late charge to the Note Holder. The amount of the charge will be **6. 00%** of my overdue payment or U.S. $5.00, which ever is more. I will pay this late charge only once on any late payment.

In the event a balloon payment is delinquent more than 10 days after the date it is due, I agree to pay a late charge in an amount equal to the maximum late charge that could have been assessed with respect to the largest single monthly installment previously due, other than the balloon payment, multiplied by the sum of one plus the number of months occurring since the late payment charge began to accrue.

(B) Default. If I do not pay the full amount of each monthly payment due under this Note by the date stated in paragraph 3 above, I will be in default, and the Note Holder may demand that I pay immediately all amounts that I owe under this Note.

Even if, at a time when I am in default, the Note Holder does not require me to pay immediately in full as described above, the Note Holder will still have the right to do so if I am in default at a later time.

(C) Payment of Note Holder's Costs and Expenses. If the Note Holder has required me to pay immediately in full as described above, the Note Holder will have the right to be paid back for all its costs and expenses to the extent not prohibited by applicable law. Those expenses include, for example, reasonable attorney's fees. A default upon any interest of any Note Holder shall be a default upon all interests.

5. BORROWER'S PAYMENTS BEFORE THEY ARE DUE - PREPAYMENT PENALTIES

I have the right to make payments of principal at any time before they are due. A payment of principal only is known as "prepayment." If I pay all or part of the loan principal before it is due, whether such payment is made voluntarily or involuntarily, I agree to pay a prepayment penalty computed as follows: **NO PREPAYMENT PENALTY.**

6. BORROWER'S WAIVERS

Applied Business Software, Inc. (800) 833-3343   Note Secured by Deed of Trust   Page 1 of 2

I waive my rights to require the Note Holder to do certain things. Those things are: (a) to demand payment of amounts due (known as "presentment"); (b) to give notice that amounts due have not been paid (known as "notice of dishonor"); (c) to obtain an official certification of nonpayment (known as "protest"). Anyone else who agrees to keep the promises made in this Note, or who agrees to make payments to the Note Holder if I fail to keep my promises under this Note, or who signs this Note to transfer it to someone else, also waives these rights. These persons are known as "guarantors, sureties and endorsers."

7. RESPONSIBILITIES OF PERSONS UNDER THIS NOTE

If more than one person signs this Note, each of us is fully and personally obligated to keep all of the promises made in this Note , including the promise to pay the full amount owed. Any person who is a guarantor, surety, or endorser of this Note is also obligated to do these things. Any person who takes over these obligations, including the obligations of the guarantor, surety, or endorser of this Note, is also obligated to keep all of the promises made in this Note. The Note Holder may enforce its rights under this Note against each person individually or against all of us together. This means that anyone of us may be required to pay all of the amounts owed under this Note.

8. THIS NOTE IS SECURED BY A DEED OF TRUST

In addition to the protection given to the Note Holder under this Note, a Deed of Trust (the "Security Instrument") with a Due-on-Transfer Clause dated the same date of this Note, protects the Note Holder from possible losses which might result if I do not keep the promises which I make in the Note. That Security Instrument describes how and under what conditions I may be required to make immediate payment in full of all amounts that I owe under this Note.

Some of those conditions are described as follows:

"Lender's Right to Require The Loan to be Paid Off Immediately. If the borrower shall sell, enter into a contract of sale, lease for a term of more than 6-years (including options to renew), lease with an option to purchase for any term, or transfer all or any part of the Property or an interest therein, excluding (a) the creation of a lien or encumbrance subordinate to this Deed of Trust, (b) or a transfer by devise, descent, or by operation of law upon the death of a joint tenant, the Lender may, at its option declare the Note and any other obligations secured by this Deed of Trust, together with accrued interest thereon, immediately due and payable, in full. No waiver of the Lender's right to accelerate shall be effective unless it is in writing."

Borrower **BOB BORROWER**	Date	Borrower	Date

ASSIGNMENT OF NOTE
SECURED BY A DEED OF TRUST

Date: _____

FOR VALUE RECEIVED, the undersigned hereby grants, assigns and transfers to:

all beneficial interest under the within Note, without recourse, and Deed of Trust securing same

_____   _____

_____   _____

DO NOT DESTROY THIS NOTE: When paid it must be surrendered to the Trustee, together with the Deed of Trust securing same for cancellation, before reconveyance will be made.

Recording Requested By
FINANCIAL TITLE COMPANY

When Recorded Mail To
J.A.FINANCIAL
301 LOS GATOS SARATOGA ROAD
SUITE A
LOS GATOS, CA. 95030

Title Order No. 1121345

Space above this line for recorder's use

DEED OF TRUST

RECORDER: INDEX FOR SPECIAL NOTICE

Loan No. 20070307

    This Deed of Trust, made this **7th** day of **March, 2007**, among the Trustor, **BOB BORROW, AN UNMARRIED** (herein "Borrower"), **FINANCIAL TITLE COMPANY** (herein "Trustee"), and the Beneficiary, **J.A. FINANCIAL,** (herein "Lender").
    The beneficiaries (or assignees) of this deed of trust have agreed in writing to be governed by the desires of the holders of more than 50% of the record beneficial interest therein with respect to actions to be taken on behalf of all holders in the event of default or foreclosure or for matters that require direction or approval of the holders, including designation of the broker, servicing agent, or other person acting on their behalf, and the sale, encumbrance or lease of real property owned by the holders resulting from foreclosure or receipt of a deed in lieu of foreclosure.

GRANT IN TRUST

BORROWER, in consideration of the indebtedness herein recited and the trust herein created, irrevocably grants, transfers, conveys and assigns to Trustee, in trust, with power of sale, the following described property located in the county of **ALAMEDA**, State of California: **LEGAL DESCRIPTION ATTACHED HERETO AND MADE PART HEREOF. APN # 123-1111-000**, which has the address of **123 ANY STREET, FREMONT CA 94539** (herein "Property Address");

    TOGETHER with all the improvements now or hereafter erected on the property, and all easements, rights, appurtenances, rents (subject however to the rights and authorities given herein to Lender to collect and apply such rents), royalties, mineral, oil and gas rights and profits, water, and water rights, and water stock, and all fixtures now or hereafter attached to the property, all of which, including replacements and additions thereto, shall be deemed to be and remain a part of the property covered by this Deed of Trust; and all of the foregoing, together with said property (or the leasehold estate if this Deed of Trust is on a leasehold) are herein referred to as the "Property";

THIS DEED OF TRUST IS MADE TO SECURE TO LENDER:
(a) the repayment of the indebtedness evidenced by Borrower's note (herein "Note") dated **March 7, 2007**, in the principal sum of U.S. **$170,000.00**, with payment of interest thereon, the payment of all other sums, with interest thereon, advanced in accordance herewith to protect the security of this Deed of Trust; the performance of the covenants and agreements of Borrower herein contained; and (b) repayment of any future advances, with interest thereon, made to the Borrower by Lender pursuant to paragraph 19 hereof (herein "Future Advances"); and in addition (c) this Deed of Trust shall provide the same security on behalf of the Lender, to cover extensions, modifications or renewals, including without limitation, extensions, modifications or renewals of the Note at a different rate of interest; and the performance of the covenants and agreements of Borrower herein contained.

    Borrower covenants that Borrower is lawfully seised of the estate hereby conveyed and has the right to grant and convey the **Property, that the Property is unencumbered except for encumbrances of record, and that Borrower will warrant and defend** generally the title to the Property against all claims and demands, subject to encumbrances of record.

UNIFORM COVENANTS. BORROWER AND LENDER COVENANT AND AGREE AS FOLLOWS:
    1. Payments of Principal and/or Interest. Borrower shall promptly pay, when due, the principal of and/or interest on the indebtedness evidenced by the Note, prepayment and late charges as provided in the Note, and the principal of and/or interest on any Future Advances secured by the Deed of Trust.
    2. Funds for Taxes and Insurance (Impounds). Subject to applicable law, and if required by the Lender, Borrower shall pay to Lender on the day monthly payments of principal and interest are payable under the Note, until the Note is paid in full, a sum (herein "Funds") equal to one-twelfth of the yearly taxes and assessments (including condominium and planned unit development

assessments, if any) which may attain priority over this Deed of Trust, and ground rents on the Property, if any, plus one-twelfth of yearly premium installments for hazard insurance, plus one-twelfth of yearly premium installments for mortgage insurance, if any, all as reasonably estimated initially and from time to time by Lender on the basis of assessments and bills and reasonable estimates thereof. Borrower shall not be obligated to make such payments of Funds to Lender to the extent that Borrower makes such payments to the holder of a prior mortgage or deed of trust if such holder is an institutional Lender.

If Borrower pays Funds to Lender, the Funds shall be held in an institution the deposits or accounts of which are insured or guaranteed by a Federal or state agency (including Lender if Lender is such an institution). Lender shall apply the Funds to pay said taxes, assessments, insurance premiums and ground rents. Lender may not charge for so holding and applying the Funds, analyzing said account or verifying and compiling said assessments and bills, unless Lender pays Borrower interest on the Funds and applicable law permits Lender to make such a charge. Borrower and Lender may agree in writing at the time of execution of this Deed of Trust that interest on the Funds shall be paid to Borrower, and unless such an agreement is made or applicable law requires such interest to be paid, Lender shall not be required to pay Borrower any interest or earnings on the Funds. Lender shall give to Borrower, without charge, an annual accounting of the Funds showing credits and debits to the Funds and the purpose for which each debit to the Funds was made. The Funds are pledged as additional security for the sums secured by this Deed of Trust.

If the amount of Funds held by Lender, together with the future monthly installments of Funds payable prior to the due dates of taxes, assessments, insurance premiums and ground rents, shall exceed the amount required to pay said taxes, assessments, insurance premiums and ground rents, such excess shall be, at Borrower's option, either promptly repaid to Borrower or credited to Borrower on monthly installments of Funds. If the amount of the Funds held by Lender shall not be sufficient to pay taxes, assessments, insurance premiums and ground rents as they fall due, Borrower shall pay to Lender any amount necessary to make up the deficiency in one or more payments as Lender may require.

Upon payment in full of all sums secured by this Deed of Trust, Lender shall promptly refund to Borrower any Funds held by Lender. If under Paragraph 18 hereof the Property is sold or the Property is otherwise acquired by Lender, Lender shall apply, no later than immediately prior to the sale of the Property or its acquisition by Lender, any Funds held by Lender at the time of application as a credit against the sums secured by this Deed of Trust.

3. Application of Payments. Unless applicable law provides otherwise, all payments received by Lender under the Note and paragraphs 1 and 2 hereof shall be applied by Lender first in payment of amounts payable to Lender by Borrower under paragraph 2 hereof, if applicable, then to interest payable on the Note, then to the principal of the Note, and then to interest and principal on any Future Advances.

4. Prior Mortgages and Deeds of Trust; Liens. Borrower shall perform all of Borrower's obligations under any mortgage, deed of trust or other security agreement with a lien which has priority over this Deed of Trust, including Borrower's covenants to make payments when due. Borrower shall pay or cause to be paid, at least 10 days before delinquency, all taxes, assessments and other charges, fines and impositions attributable to the Property which may attain a priority over this Deed of Trust, and leasehold payments or ground rents, if any.

5. Hazard Insurance. Borrower agrees to provide, maintain and deliver to Lender fire insurance satisfactory and with loss payable to Lender. The amount collected under any fire or other insurance policy may be applied by Lender upon any indebtedness secured hereby and in such order as Lender may determine, or at option of Lender the entire amount so collected or any part thereof may be released to the Borrower. Such application or release shall not cure or waive any Default or Notice of Default hereunder or invalidate any act done pursuant to such notice.

The insurance carrier providing the insurance shall be chosen by Borrower subject to approval by Lender; provided that such approval shall not be unreasonably withheld. All insurance policies and renewals thereof shall be in a form acceptable to Lender and shall include a standard mortgage clause in favor of and in a form acceptable to Lender. Lender shall have the right to hold the policies and renewals thereof, subject to the terms of any mortgage, deed of trust or other security agreement with a lien which has priority over this Deed of Trust.

In the event of a loss, Borrower shall give prompt notice to the insurance carrier and Lender. Lender may make proof of loss if not made promptly by Borrower.

If the Property is abandoned by Borrower, or if Borrower fails to respond to Lender within 30 days from the date notice is mailed by Lender to Borrower that the insurance carrier offers to settle a claim for insurance benefits, Lender is authorized to collect and apply their insurance proceeds at Lender's option either to restoration or repair of the Property or to the sums secured by this Deed of Trust.

If Borrower obtains earthquake, flood or any other hazard insurance, or any other insurance on the Property, and such insurance is not specifically required by the Lender, then such insurance shall: (i) name the Lender as loss payee thereunder, and (ii) be subject to all of the provisions of this paragraph 5.

6. Preservation and Maintenance of Property; Leaseholds; Condominiums; Planned Unit Developments. Borrower shall keep the Property in good repair and shall not commit waste or permit impairment or deterioration of the Property and shall comply with the provisions of any lease if this Deed of Trust is on a leasehold. If this Deed of Trust is on a unit in a condominium or a planned unit development, Borrower shall perform all of Borrower's obligations under the declaration of covenants creating or governing the condominium or planned unit development, the by-laws and regulations of the condominium or planned unit development, and constituent documents.

7. Protection of Lender's Security. If Borrower fails to perform the covenants and agreements contained in this Deed of Trust, or if any action or proceeding is commenced which affects Lender's interest in the Property, including but not limited to proceedings by the Lender to obtain relief from stay in any bankruptcy proceeding which would prohibit Lender enforcing its rights under the Deed of Trust, then Lender, at Lender's option, may make such appearances, disburse such sums, including reasonable attorney's fees, and take such action as is necessary to protect Lender's interest. If Lender required mortgage insurance as a condition of making the loan secured by this Deed of Trust, Borrower shall pay the premiums required to maintain such insurance in effect until such time as the requirement for such insurance terminates in accordance with Borrower's and Lender's written agreement or applicable law.

Any amounts disbursed by Lender pursuant to this paragraph 7, with interest thereon, including but not limited to payment of delinquent taxes and assessments, insurance premiums due, and delinquent amounts owed to prior lien holders, shall become additional indebtedness of Borrower secured by this Deed of Trust . Such amounts as are disbursed by Lender shall be payable, upon notice from Lender to Borrower requesting payment thereof, and shall bear interest from the date of disbursement at the rate payable on the Note. Nothing contained in this paragraph 7 shall require Lender to incur any expense or take any action hereunder.

8. Inspection. Lender may make or cause to be made reasonable entries upon and inspection of the Property, provided that Lender shall give Borrower notice prior to any such inspection specifying reasonable cause therefore related to Lender's interest in the Property.

9. Condemnation. The proceeds of any award or claim for damages, direct or consequential, in conjunction with any condemnation or other taking of the Property, or part thereof, or for conveyance in lieu of condemnation, are hereby assigned and shall be paid to Lender, subject to the terms of any mortgage, deed of trust or other security agreement with a lien which has priority over this Deed of Trust.

10. Borrower Not Released. At any time or from time to time, without liability therefore and without notice upon written request of Lender and presentation of this Deed and said Note for endorsement, and without affecting the personal liability of any person for payment of the indebtedness secured hereby, Trustee may: reconvey any part of said property; consent to the making of any map or plat thereof; join in granting any easement thereon; or join in any extension agreement or any agreement subordinating the lien or charge thereof. Trustee may, but shall be under no obligation or duty to, appear in or defend any action or proceeding purporting to affect said property or the title thereto, or purporting to affect the security hereof or the rights or powers of Lender or Trustee.

11. Forbearance by Lender Not a Waiver. Any forbearance by Lender in exercising any right or remedy hereunder, or otherwise afforded by applicable law, shall not be a waiver of or preclude the exercise of any such right or remedy. The procurement of insurance or the payment of taxes or other liens or charges by Lender shall not be a waiver of Lender's right to accelerate the maturity of the indebtedness secured by this Deed of Trust.

12. Remedies Cumulative. All remedies provided in this Deed of Trust are distinct and cumulative to any other or remedy under this Deed of Trust or afforded by law or equity, and may be exercised concurrently, independently or successively.

13. Successors and Assigns Bound; Joint and Several Liability; Co-signers. The covenants and agreements herein contained shall bind, and the rights hereunder shall inure to, the respective successors and assigns of Lender and Borrower, subject to the provisions of paragraph 18 hereof. All covenants and agreements of Borrower shall be joint and several.

14. Notice. Except for any notice required under applicable law to be given in another manner, (a) any notice to Borrower provided for in this Deed of Trust shall be given by delivering it or by mailing such notice by certified mail addressed to Borrower or the Property at the Property Address or at such other address as Borrower may designate by notice to Lender as provided herein, and (b) any notice to Lender shall be given by certified mail to Lender, in care of Lender's Servicing Agent ("Agent"), **J.A. FINANCIAL 301 LOS GATOS SARATOGA ROAD, LOS GATOS, CA. 95030** or to such other address as Lender or Agent may designate by notice to Borrower as provided herein. Any notice provided for in this Deed of Trust shall be deemed to have been given to Borrower or Lender when given in the manner designated herein.

15. This Deed of Trust shall be governed by the Laws of the State of California. In the event that any provision or clause of this Deed of Trust or the Note conflicts with applicable law, such conflict shall not effect other provisions of this Deed of Trust or the Note which can be given effect without the conflicting provision, and to this end the provisions of the Deed of Trust are declared to be severable.

16. Lender's Right to Require The Loan to be Paid Off Immediately. If the Borrower shall sell, enter into a contract of sale, lease for a term of more than 6-years (including options to renew), lease with an option to purchase for any term, or transfer all or any part of the Property or an interest therein, excluding (a) the creation of a lien or encumbrance subordinate to this Deed of Trust, (b) or a transfer by devise, descent, or by operation of law upon the death of a joint tenant, the Lender may, at its option declare the Note and any other obligations secured by this Deed of Trust, together with accrued interest thereon, immediately due and payable, in full. No waiver or the Lender's right to accelerate shall be effective unless it is in writing.

If Lender exercises such option to accelerate, Lender shall mail Borrower notice of acceleration in accordance with paragraph 14 hereof. Such notice shall provide a period of not less than 30 days from the date the notice is mailed within which Borrower may pay the sums declared due. If Borrower fails to pay such sums prior to the expiration of such period, Lender may, without further notice or demand on Borrower, invoke any remedies permitted by paragraph 17 hereof.

BORROWER AND LENDER FURTHER COVENANT AND AGREE AS FOLLOWS:

17. Assignment of Rents; Appointment of Receiver; Lender in Possession. As additional security hereunder, and without regard to the adequacy of any security for the indebtedness hereby secured, Borrower hereby assigns to Lender the rents of the

Property, provided that Borrower shall, prior to acceleration under paragraph 18 hereof or abandonment of the Property, have the right to collect and retain such rents as they become due and payable.

Upon acceleration under paragraph 18 hereof or abandonment of the Property, Lender, in person, by Agent or by judicially appointed receiver shall be entitled to enter upon, take possession of and manage the Property and to collect the rents of the Property including those past due. All rents collected by Lender or the receiver shall be applied first to payment of the costs of management of the Property and collection of rents, including, but not limited to, receiver's fees, premiums on receiver's bonds and reasonable attorney's fees, and then to the sums secured by this Deed of Trust. Lender and the receiver shall be liable to account only for those rents actually received.

18. Upon default by Borrower in payment of any indebtedness secured hereby or in performance of any agreement hereunder, Lender may declare all sums secured hereby immediately due and payable by delivery to Trustee of written declaration of default and demand for sale and of written Notice of Default and of election to cause to be sold said property, which notice Trustee shall cause to be filed for record. Trustee shall be entitled to rely upon the correctness of such notice. Lender also shall deposit with Trustee this Deed, said Note and all documents evidencing expenditures secured hereby.

After the lapse of such time as then may be required by law following the recordation of said Notice of Default and Notice of Sale having been given as then required by law, Trustee, without demand on Trustor, shall sell said property at the time and place fixed by it in said Notice of Sale, either as a whole or in separate parcels and in such order as it may determine (but subject to any statutory right of Trustor to direct the order in which said property, if consisting of several lots or parcels, shall be sold), at public auction to the highest bidder for cash in lawful money of the United States, payable at time of sale. Trustee may postpone sale of all or any portion of said property by public announcement at such time and place of sale, and from time to time thereafter may postpone such sale by public announcement at the time fixed by the preceding postponement. Trustee shall deliver to such purchaser its deed conveying the property to sold, but without any covenant or warranty, expressed or implied. The recitals in such deed of any matters or facts shall be conclusive proof of the truthfulness thereof. Any person including Trustor, Trustee, or Beneficiary as hereinafter defined, may purchase at such sale.

After deducting all costs, fees and expenses of Trustee and of this Trust, including cost of evidence of title in connection with sale, Trustee shall apply the proceeds of sale to payment of; all sums expended under the terms hereof, not then repaid, with accrued interest at the rate prescribed in the Note; all other sums then secured thereby; and the remainder, if any, to the person or persons legally entitled thereto.

19. **Future Advances.** Upon request of Borrower, Lender, at Lender's option prior to full reconveyance of the Property by Trustee to Borrower, may make Future Advances to Borrower. Such advances with interest thereon, shall be secured by this Deed of Trust when evidenced by promissory notes stating that said notes are secured hereby.

20. **Reconveyance.** Upon written request of Lender stating that all sums secured hereby have been paid, and upon surrender of this Deed and said Note to Trustee for cancellation and retention and upon payment of its fees, Trustee shall reconvey, without warranty, the property then held hereunder. The recitals in such reconveyance of any matters or facts shall be conclusive proof of the truthfulness thereof. The grantee in such reconveyance may be described as "the person or persons legally entitled thereto." The Trustee may destroy said Note, this Deed or Trust (and any other documents related thereto) upon the first to occur of the following: 5 years after issuance of a full reconveyance; or, recordation of the Note and Deed of Trust in a form or medium which permits their reproduction for 5 years following issuance of a full reconveyance.

21. **Substitution of Trustee.** Lender, at Lender's option, may from time to time remove Trustee and appoint a successor trustee to any Trustee appointed hereunder. Without conveyance of the Property, the successor trustee shall succeed to all the title, power and duties conferred upon the Trustee herein and by applicable law.

22. **Request for Notices.** Borrower requests that copies of the notice of sale and notice of default be sent to Borrower's address which is the Property Address.

23. **Statement of Obligation.** Lender may collect a fee, not to exceed the maximum amount permitted by law, for furnishing the statement of obligations as provided by Section 2943 of the Civil Code of California.

MISCELLANEOUS PROVISIONS

24. **Construction or Home Improvement Loan.** If the loan secured by this Deed of Trust is a construction or home improvement loan, Borrower is required to perform according to the terms and conditions of each agreement contained in any building, home improvement or similar agreement between the Borrower and Lender.

25. **Acceptance by Lender of a Partial Payment After Notice of Default.** By accepting partial payment (payments which do not satisfy a default or delinquency in full) of any sums secured by this Deed of Trust after a Notice of Default has been recorded, or by accepting late performance of any obligation secured by this Deed of Trust, or by adding any payment so made to the loan secured by this Deed of Trust, whether or not such payments are made pursuant to a court order, the Lender does not waive its right either to require prompt payment when due of all other sums so secured or to declare default for failure to make any such prompt payment or to perform any such act. No exercise of any right or remedy of the Lender or Trustee under this Deed of Trust shall constitute a waiver of any other right or remedy contained in this Deed of Trust or provided by law.

**REQUEST FOR SPECIAL NOTICE OF DEFAULT AND FORECLOSURE
UNDER SUPERIOR MORTGAGES OR DEEDS OF TRUST**

Applied Business Software, Inc. (800) 833-3343

In accordance with Section 2924b of the Civil Code, Request is hereby made by the undersigned Trustor that a copy of any default and a copy of any notice of sale under deed of trust recorded in Book _____, Page(s) _____, Instrument No._____, Official Records of County Recorder of _____ County, California. The original Trustor _____ and the original Trustee _____ and the original Beneficiary _____ Mail to:

IN WITNESS WHEREOF, BORROWER HAS EXECUTED THIS DEED OF TRUST

| Borrower | *BOB BORROWER* | Date | Borrower | Date |

State of California
County of
On _____ before me, _____, personally appeared

personally known to me (or proved to me on the basis of satisfactory evidence) to be the person(s) whose name(s) subscribed to the within instrument and acknowledged to me that _____ executed the same in _____ authorized capacity(ies), and that by _____ signature(s) on the instrument the person(s), or the entity upon behalf of which the person(s) acted, executed the instrument.

WITNESS my hand and official seal.

Signature _____   (Seal)

REQUEST FOR FULL RECONVEYANCE

The undersigned is the holder of the note or notes secured by this Deed of Trust. Said note or notes, together with all **other indebtedness secured by this Deed of Trust, have been paid in full. You are hereby directed to cancel said note or notes and this Deed of Trust, which are delivered hereby, and to reconvey, without warranty,** all the estate now held by you under this Deed of Trust to the person or persons legally entitled thereto.

Signature of Beneficiary (the "LENDER")   Date   Signature of Beneficiary (the "LENDER")   Date

When recorded, mail to

Att: _____

RECORDING REQUESTED BY

AND WHEN RECORDED MAIL TO

Name

Street
Address

City,State
Zip

Order No. _____

APN No:

Request for Notice Under Section 2924b Civil Code

In accordance with Section 2924b, Civil Code, request is hereby made that a copy of any Notice of Default and a copy of any Notice of Sale under the Deed of Trust recorded as Instrument No. _____, on

_____ in Book _____, Page _____ of Official Records of

_____ County, California

executed by _____, as Trustor

in which _____ is named as

Beneficiary, and _____

as TRUSTEE, be mailed to _____

at _____

NOTICE: A copy of any Notice of Default and any Notice of Sale will be sent only to the address contained in this recorded Request: If your address changes, a new Request must be recorded.

Dated: March 1, 2007

STATE OF CALIFORNIA
COUNTY OF_____   S.S. _____

On _____ before me,   _____

_____   _____

a Notary Public, personally appeared   _____

_____

_____   _____

personally known to me (or proved to me on the basis of satisfactory evidence) to be the person(s) whose name(s) is/are subscribed to the within instrument and acknowledged to me that he/she/they executed the same in his/her/their authorized capacity(ies) and that by his/her/their signature(s) on the instrument the person(s), or the entity upon behalf of which the person(s), acted, executed the instrument.

WITNESS my hand and official seal.

Signature _____

(This area for official notorial seal)

Rqnotice (rev. 12/28/05)

Make Your Money Make Money For You

Recording Requested By
ABC TITLE COMPANY

When Recorded Mail To
MIKE INVESTOR
123 ABC STREET
SAN JOSE, CA. 11111

Title Order No. 1415678

Space above this line for recorder's use

REQUEST FOR WRITTEN NOTICE OF DELINQUENCIES
PURSUANT TO CIVIL CODE SECTION 2924e

Date:	**March 1, 2007**	Your Loan No.:	**20072020**
To:	**SENIOR LENDER**	Property Address:	**111 ABC STREET, ANY TOWN, CA 91111**
		Trustor(s):	**BOB BORROWER**

In accordance with Section 2924e of the Civil Code, request is hereby made by the undersigned trustor(s) that you provide written notice of any and all delinquencies of four months or more, whether or not a Notice of Default is recorded, under your deed of trust recorded as instrument number **123456**, Official Records of County Recorder of **CONTRA COSTA** County, the original Trustor(s) **BOB BORROWER** and the original Beneficiary **SENIOR LENDER**. Mail the written notice as referenced above to **MIKE INVESTOR 123 ABC STREET, SAN JOSE, CA. 11111** on behalf of **MIKE INVESTOR** (hereinafter "REQUESTER") who is the beneficiary of a loan in the principal amount of **$100,000.00** made to the above named trustor(s). Said loan is secured by a deed of trust junior to your loan as referenced hereinabove. The term of the aforementioned loan is for **61 months**, beginning on **May 1, 2007** and becoming due and payable in full on **May 1, 2012** (maturity date). As provided by law, the fee for this service is $40.00, which amount is enclosed herein.

I (we) do hereby consent to your providing the above described information to or to the order of REQUESTER with reference to the loan wherein your firm is either beneficiary or servicing agent.

Borrower	*BOB BORROWER*	Date	
Borrower		Date	

State of California
County of
On _____ before me, _____ , personally appeared _____

personally known to me (or proved to me on the basis of satisfactory evidence) to be the person(s) whose name(s) subscribed
to the within instrument and acknowledged to me that _____ executed the same in _____ authorized
capacity(ies), and that by _____ signature(s) on the instrument the person(s), or the entity upon behalf
of which the person(s) acted, executed the instrument.

WITNESS my hand and official seal.

_____
Signature   (Seal)

Applied Business Software, Inc. (800) 833-3343

[41186395/ROAY]
Request For Written Notice of Delinquencies   Page 1 of 1

GLOSSARY OF TERMS

ACCELERATION CLAUSE: If a home owner sells, transfers, or changes the title to the property, the entire loan balance will immediately come due, regardless of the original terms of the loan.

ACCRUED INTEREST: The interest earned on a Note, but, not yet received.

ACKNOWLEDGEMENT: In California, any document that needs to be recorded must be notarized. The person who signs the document in the presence of a notary public, in fact acknowledges, that he signed the said document.

ADVANCE FEE: Some Notes have a clause that enables the investor to collect an advance fee on the amounts advanced. This would be done to reinstate senior loans or to bring real estate taxes current. Generally, such a fee is about 2% of the money advanced.

ALIENATION CLAUSE: Similar to an acceleration clause, except, it specifically refers to a situation when the title changes hands. The loan balance will then immediately come due.

ALL INCLUSIVE DEED OF TRUST (AITD): Where the seller carries back a Note that wraps around the existing encumbrances on the property. The buyer makes the payment on the total loans on the property to the seller, or, the owner of the AITD and the seller then turns around, and makes the payment to the lender(s). Very few title companies deal with wrap arounds.

ALTA TITLE INSURANCE POLICY: ALTA stands for "American Land Title Insurance Association." It's a policy that covers items found in county records, and items discovered by the physical inspection of the property.

AMORTIZED: If a loan is amortized over a certain period of time, it means that the payments consist of both the principal and interest. At the end of the loan term, the balance will be zero. There are also partially amortized loans that involve a balloon payment at the end of a specific number of years. An amortized payment always includes interest. A *negative amortization* is where the loan payment is less than the interest, making the principal balance of the loan grow.

ANNUAL PERCENTAGE RATE (APR): APR is calculated by taking into account the interest rate, loan fees, and the term of the loan.

APPRAISAL: It is an estimate of the market value of the property at a certain date. Such estimation is generally called an "appraised value."

APPRAISER: An appraiser is a professional who is certified by the State to do property appraisals.

ARREARS: If your loan is funded on December 31, your first payment will be due on February 1, meaning that the January interest will be paid in February, or in arrears. As an example, the rent is always paid in advance, but, the interest is always paid in arrears. The term "arrears" is also used in lieu of past due payments. For instance, instead of being two months past due on your payments, one can say, the payments are two months in arrears.

ASSIGNEE: The person who receives the title to a note from the present Note holder is the assignee.

ASSIGNMENT: When the rights of one Note holder are assigned to another, it is called "assignment."

ASSIGNOR: It refers to the person who is assigning the Note to the other (assignee).

ASSUMPTION: Sometimes a new buyer wants to take over the existing loan on a property. When the new homebuyer does it formally, meeting all the requirements of the lender, it's called an assumption.

BACK PAYMENTS: Past due payments.

BALLOON PAYMENT: A lump sum payment of principal and interest to pay off the loan, in full, is called a balloon payment. There could also be partial balloon payments. For example, there could be a clause that the borrower will pay $30,000, at the end of three years, and the entire remaining principal and interest balance, at the end of five years.

BENEFICIARY: The one who receives the payments; the lender, in most cases, or, its assignee.

CALIFORNIA LAND TITLE ASSOCIATION (CLTA) POLICY: This is also referred to as "standard title insurance policy," and covers everything about the property that can be discovered through the County Recorder's office.

CARRY BACK: When a property seller carries back part of the sale price, in the form of a Mortgage or Trust Deed Note, it is referred to as carrying back.

CASH-ON-CASH-BASIS: Cash return, not factoring in tax liabilities or benefits.

CLEAN PRELIM: A Title Report that has no delinquent taxes and no judgments showing. It shows only what it's supposed to show.

CLOSING: It refers to closing a transaction or closing *escrow*. "Closing statement" is a popular term in the loan industry, as it tells how much the property was sold for and the exchange of cash.

COLLATERAL: Another word for security. The borrower's house is the collateral for this loan.

CO-BORROWER: A spouse is a co-borrower. A parent or another person can also co-sign and become a co-borrower.

COMPARABLES (COMPS): Comparing the property to other similar sold properties in the immediate neighborhood, within the last six months. Such properties are referred to as comps or comparables.

COMPOUND INTEREST: When interest earned is added on to the principal amount and starts earning interest.

CONSTRUCTIVE NOTICE: When a deed is recorded, it is assumed that everyone knows about it.

CREDITOR: The lender, or the person to whom debt is owed.

DEBT RATIO (DR): Most all banks and other financial institutions use debt ratio to qualify a borrower. The debt ratio is mostly based on the gross monthly income of the borrower(s) and could be as high as 60%, depending on the strength of the borrower and the financial institution doing the loan. Sixty percent debt ratio would mean that if the borrower makes $1000 gross a month, his total monthly expenses should not be more than $600 a month.

DEBTOR: A borrower. One who owes.

DEED OF TRUST: A security instrument, securing the Promissory Note. The Deed of Trust, which is recorded with the County Recorder's office, has three parties to it: The lender or beneficiary, the borrower or trustor, and a third, neutral party called the trustee. In a Deed of Trust, the trustor gives power to the trustee to foreclose on the loan if he defaults, or, to reconvey the deed, once the loan is paid off.

DEFAULT: Violation of the terms or the conditions of the Note or the Deed of Trust.

DELINQUENCY: It refers to past due or delinquent loan payments.

DEMAND FOR PAY-OFF: A written statement from the investor stating the dollar amount it will take to pay-off the loan by a certain date.

DISCOUNT: The difference between the price paid and the face value of a Note.

ENCUMBRANCE: The lien, whether voluntary or involuntary, on a property, is called an encumbrance.

EQUITY: The difference between the market value of a property and what is owed against it.

ESCROW: A neutral third party, who sees that the conditions and the terms of the contract, of both parties (borrower and lender), are met.

FIRST TRUST DEED: The first in line of recorded Trust Deeds on a property.

FORECLOSURE: When the trustor is behind in loan payments, the lender can enforce his right to payment by foreclosing on the property. Once the foreclosure proceedings have started, the borrower has three months in which to bring the loan current. There is also a judicial foreclosure through the court.

HAZARD INSURANCE: It is the same as homeowner's insurance, which covers the property owner (and the lender(s)) against losses by fire. Flood and earthquake insurance, if applicable, provide the same protection against losses incurred by flood and earthquake. Be sure to read the deductibles on flood and earthquake insurance policies.

HYPOTHECATION: Putting an asset as a security for a loan. You can hypothecate a Trust Deed Note, that is, you can place your Note as a security for a loan against it.

INSTRUMENT: Any document proving a debt or other legal agreement.

INSURANCE LOSS PAYEE: This is an insurance policy that a homeowner obtains from their insurance company. It lists the lender as the *loss payee* on the policy. For instance, if the house burned down, the policy would cover the investor, up to the insured amount.

INTEREST ONLY: No money is being applied toward the principal.

JUNIOR LIEN: Any Trust Deed or Mortgage recorded *after* the First Deed of Trust is a junior lien. If there are three Trust Deeds, then the third is junior to the Second and first mortgages.

LEGAL DESCRIPTION: The County Recorder's office files data relating to, and identifying properties, by an assessor's parcel number, book number, page number, and tract number.

Such description is referred to as a legal description.

LENDABLE EQUITY: The maximum loan that a lender or investor will lend on a property. Let's say that the property value is $100,000. The investor will not likely go more than 75% LTV. The first mortgage balance is $50,000. 75% of $100,000 is $75,000. Minus the first mortgage of $50,000 and you have a lendable equity of $25,000, even though the equity is $50,000.

LIEN: A recorded Trust Deed is a lien. Any encumbrance, voluntary and involuntary, is a lien.

LIS PENDENCE: A legal term meaning an action is pending. When someone sues another person over a piece of real estate, they will put a *lis pendence* on the defendant's property that is the subject of the law suit. It means that the defendant cannot sell the property until the lawsuit is settled

LOAN TO VALUE RATIO (LTV): LTV is used to determine the risk factor of a Trust Deed loan. The ratio is calculated by adding all the loans against a property; including the one you are about to make, and dividing the total amount by the property value.

MORTGAGE: It's a security instrument by which the property is pledged, to insure payment of a loan. It differs from a Trust Deed in that; a foreclosure on a mortgage would have to go through the court system. A trust deed does not have to go through the court.

MORTGAGEE: It is another term for a beneficiary or lender.

MORTGAGOR: The person borrowing the loan. Also known as a debtor or trustor.

MORTGAGE RATING: It shows how the borrower pays on his mortgage. It also shows the date the mortgage was originated; the original loan amount; the present balance; the interest rate; the monthly payment; how many late charges, if any, the borrower has incurred in last twelve months, etc.

NOTICE OF DEFAULT: It is a notice given to the borrower and to all the junior lien holders informing them that the loan is in default, and foreclosure proceedings have started.

NOTICE OF DELINQUENCY: This notice informs the junior lien holders that the borrower is past due on the senior loan payment(s). The notice is given to junior lien holders only if they've filed a request for one.

NOTICE OF TRUSTEE'S SALE: This is a notice about the pending sale of a property in foreclosure. Such a notice is published in a newspaper of general circulation, in the county where the property is located.

PAYOR: The person who makes the payments on the Note.

PAYEE: The person to whom payments are due on a Note.

PITI: It's short for "principal, interest, taxes and insurance."

POINTS: The loan origination fee charged by the broker and the lender, is referred to as, points. One point is equal to one percent of the loan amount.

PRECEDENCE: Priority. The first mortgage loan, because it was there prior to the Second Trust Deed, would take precedence over the Second Trust Deed.

PRELIMINARY TITLE REPORT (PRELIM): Issued by a Title Company, a prelim discloses all the liens on a property, as well as, information on who owns the title, whether there's a notice of default, and if real estate taxes have been paid.

PREPAYMENT PENALTY: Some Notes have clauses that state that if the borrower pays off the loan, prior to a certain specified date; he'll be charged a certain amount of interest as a prepayment penalty. The prepayment penalty is never more than six months interest on 80% of the principal balance.

RECISSION NOTICE: This notice means that a borrower has three days to think about a loan and has the right to cancel it without any obligation. Some lenders will let the borrower waive the three-day rescission notice, if they receive a written request to waive the rescission period, for reasons of financial distress.

REFINANCE: When a property owner takes out a new mortgage loan to pay off an existing loan, it's called a refinance. It is different from a home equity loan, in which the original first mortgage loan stays intact.

REINSTATEMENT PERIOD: This is a period, generally up to five days before the auction, in which the borrower has the right to bring the loan current, thereby, reinstating the loan.

STRAIGHT NOTE: A Note that has no payments. Both, principal and interest are due at the end of the loan term

TITLE: "Title" refers to the legal ownership vested in the property owner.

TITLE INSURANCE: Issued by the Title Company and paid by the borrower, the title insurance guarantees that the title to the property is vested in the borrower and that the only liens against the property are those that appear in the Title Report. It insures the investor for the full amount of the investment.

TITLE POLICY ENDORSEMENT: It's faster and cheaper to roll over ownership of an existing title policy, than it is to obtain a new one. A Title Policy Endorsement is needed when a broker or a lender assigns the Note to a new investor.

TRUSTEE: A neutral third party, who handles the title transaction, and is also vested with the power to foreclose, in case of default.

TRUSTOR: The borrower. The one who receives the loan and makes the payments.

USURY: Usury laws limit the interest a person can charge. There is no usury for Mortgage Brokers in the State of California, and none, if you are buying a Note from a Mortgage Broker.

YIELD: This is the effective return on a Note. It's generally higher than the interest rate because of other factors, such as discounting and prepayment penalty.

Made in the USA
Lexington, KY
07 May 2011